Opting Out

OPTING OUT

Conscience and Cooperation in a Pluralistic Society

DAVID S. ODERBERG

Institute of
Economic Affairs

First published in Great Britain in 2018 by
The Institute of Economic Affairs
2 Lord North Street
Westminster
London SW1P 3LB
in association with London Publishing Partnership Ltd
www.londonpublishingpartnership.co.uk

The mission of the Institute of Economic Affairs is to improve understanding
of the fundamental institutions of a free society by analysing and expounding
the role of markets in solving economic and social problems.

A CIP catalogue record for this book is available from the British Library.

ISBN 978-0-255-36761-5

Many IEA publications are translated into languages other
than English or are reprinted. Permission to translate or to reprint
should be sought from the Director General at the address above.

Typeset in Kepler by T&T Productions Ltd
www.tandtproductions.com

Printed and bound in Great Britain by Hobbs the Printers Ltd

CONTENTS

THE AUTHOR

David S. Oderberg is Professor of Philosophy at the University of Reading. He completed his doctorate at Wolfson College, Oxford, and became Lecturer in Philosophy at Reading in 1992. He has written four books and edited or co-edited five others, as well as being the author of over sixty papers. His main research areas are metaphysics and ethics, but he also works in philosophy of religion, philosophy of science, and other areas. In 2013 he delivered the Hourani Lectures in Ethics at the State University of New York, Buffalo, and in 2003 was a Visiting Scholar at the Social Philosophy and Policy Center, Bowling Green, Ohio. Professor Oderberg is a Senior Fellow of the Higher Education Academy, and in 2016 was named, by a major US website for prospective college applicants, as one of the fifty most influential living philosophers.

ACKNOWLEDGEMENTS

I am grateful to Philip Booth for commissioning this monograph on behalf of the IEA, and to his successor, Jamie Whyte, for seeing it through to publication. Philip and I had some very interesting initial discussions on some of the topics presented here, and I am delighted that he found those topics sufficiently important to be worth examining in this short work. I also thank audiences at the University of Buckingham and St Mary's University, Twickenham, to whom I presented some of this material. Further thanks are due to an anonymous referee who made many constructive comments that have improved this monograph. I would also like to thank Jon Wainwright for his expert editing and assistance, not to mention his patience and good cheer, as the final copy was prepared. In addition, I am grateful to the University of Reading for its support in enabling me to complete this work in a timely manner.

SUMMARY

We live in a liberal, pluralistic, largely secular society where, in theory, there is fundamental protection for freedom of conscience generally and freedom of religion in particular. There is, however, both in statute and common law, increasing pressure on religious believers and conscientious objectors (outside wartime) to act in ways that violate their sincere, deeply held beliefs. This is particularly so in health care, where conscientious objection is coming under extreme pressure. I argue that freedom of religion and conscience need to be put on a sounder footing both legislatively and by the courts, particularly in health care. I examine a number of important legal cases in the UK and US, where freedom of religion and conscience have come into conflict with government mandates or equality and anti-discrimination law. In these and other cases we find one of two results: either the conscientious objector loses out against competing rights, or the conscientious objector succeeds, but due to what I consider unsound judicial reasoning. In particular, cases involving *cooperation* in what the objector considers morally impermissible according to their beliefs have been wrongly understood by some American courts. I argue that a reasonable theory of cooperation incorporated into judicial thinking would enable more acceptable results that gave sufficient protection to conscientious objectors without risking a judicial backlash against objectors who wanted to take their freedoms too far.

I also venture into broader, more controversial waters concerning what I call *freedom of dissociation* – the fundamental right to withdraw from associating with people, groups, and activities. It is no more than the converse of freedom of association, which all free societies recognise as a basic right. How far should freedom of dissociation go? What might society be like if freedom of dissociation were given more protection in law than it currently has? It would certainly give freedom of religion and conscience a substantial foundation, but it could also lead to discriminatory behaviour to which many people would object. I explore some of these issues, before going back to the narrower area of freedom of conscience and religion in health care, making some proposals about how the law could strengthen these basic pillars of a liberal, free society.

1 INTRODUCTION

Brief background to this book

What threats are there to freedom in contemporary Western societies? Many of us would immediately think of such things as terrorism, mass surveillance or the general power of an overweening state. All of these are serious concerns, no doubt. There is, however, a threat that is in some ways more insidious or less overt – until one finds oneself facing it. This is the threat to freedom of conscience and, more specifically, freedom of religion.

Most of the cases we will look at involve the threat to freedom of religion, but the danger applies equally to the more general freedom of conscience. I will take some liberty on occasion in using the terms interchangeably, sometimes also using one of the terms to refer broadly to both kinds of freedom. When we think of freedom of religion, we often think of the freedom publicly to profess one's faith and to live according to one's religious tenets without fear of persecution or repression by the state or one's fellow citizens. In this monograph, however, I will consider a narrower aspect of freedom of religion, one that brings out its relationship to freedom of conscience. At its core, freedom of religion involves the right to live according to one's sincerely held religious beliefs, at least the tenets making up the essence of the religious system to which a person adheres. This cannot, of course, be an unqualified right, and we will look at difficult cases as we go along. One thing we can be fairly certain of, though: in a society professing itself to be liberal and tolerant, compelling or coercing religious believers to act in ways *contrary* to their sincere, core beliefs should form no part of law or public policy except in the most extreme cases – cases about which no reasonable person, religious or not, could disagree.

Freedom of conscience might not involve religious beliefs; it arises also in the case of non-believers and people who are generally opposed to religion. In all cases, though, it will involve some deeply held beliefs of an ethical nature. A conscientious objector in wartime, for example, might be a pacifist for non-religious reasons, but liberal societies have typically allowed such a person to live according to their pacifism by assigning them in wartime to non-combat duties such as medicine or administration, or even allowing them to abstain from any involvement in the war effort.

If freedom of religion and conscience mean anything in a liberal society, it must mean the right at least to live out one's core beliefs in a way that does not involve compulsion to violate them, whether it be the threat of force, the imposition of significant material burdens, and the like. Even if one puts aside behaviour such as public profession, proselytisation, political activism, and so on, it remains that not being compelled to violate one's beliefs is a *sine qua non* of religious freedom in a liberal society. Freedom of religion and conscience have typically involved these other activities as well, but I am concerned with the narrower core. That core must entail a person's freedom from being *coerced* by the state to violate their deeply held beliefs. Rightly do we balk at the very idea that a government could *force* by law, threat, or actual violence, a Christian or a Jew, say, publicly to denounce their faith, or prevent them from attending a place of worship, or from speaking openly about their religion. The same for compelling a pacifist to serve on the front line, or a vegetarian to eat meat. These, we believe, are the hallmarks of totalitarianism.

Fortunately, Western societies have not *yet* reached that stage. We are, however, moving in a direction uncomfortably close to that sort of coercion, so far confined to the legal system. Consider some recent news stories:

(1) Health insurers in California have been *required* by the state to provide health cover for abortion (not just contraception) *even if* the employer is a *church*.[1]

(2) The College of Physicians and Surgeons of Ontario, Canada, now requires all Ontario doctors to *refer* requesters of euthanasia if the doctor objects.[2]

(3) A Catholic care home in Belgium has been *fined* for refusing euthanasia.[3]

---

1 http://www.catholicherald.co.uk/news/2016/06/23/california-churches-forced-to-cover-abortion-in-healthcare-plans/ [last accessed 19.10.17].

2 http://www.nationalreview.com/corner/437649/ontario-md-assoc-requires-all-docs-complicity-euthananasia [sic; last accessed 19.10.17].

3 http://www.catholicherald.co.uk/news/2016/07/04/catholic-care-home-in-belgium-fined-for-refusing-euthanasia/ [last accessed 19.10.17].

Cases such as these are arising ever more regularly in the field of health care. Moreover, fifteen philosophers and bioethicists recently issued a 'consensus statement' stating that conscientious objection should be all but *eliminated* from health care (Uehiro 2016). They say that 'the patient's wellbeing (or best interest, or health)' should 'normally take priority over [a health care practitioner's] personal moral or religious views'. If a practitioner has a conscientious objection to providing some treatment or procedure, they must always refer the patient to someone who will provide it. They must 'explain the rationale' for their objection to a 'tribunal'. If the objector receives an exemption, they must 'compensate society and the health system for their failure to fulfil their professional obligations by providing public-benefitting services.' Medical students should receive *no* exemption from learning how to perform procedures they believe to be morally wrong. Health care practitioners should be 'educated to reflect on the influence of cognitive bias in their objections'.

Such an extreme statement, albeit by only a handful of academics, is disturbing – the sort of thing one might expect from a totalitarian regime rather than a liberal society that professed respect for diverse religious and ethical beliefs. As John Rawls, a key apostle of liberalism, affirms: 'reasonable persons will think it unreasonable to use political power, should they possess it, to repress comprehensive views that are not unreasonable, though different from their own' (Rawls 1993: 60). Needless to say, assessing what counts as reasonable is of central importance – obviously a task well beyond the scope of this small monograph, especially if we are thinking 'cosmically', as it were, about reasonable and unreasonable views of the world, ethical and religious systems, and so on. That aside, however, must we agree that opposition to euthanasia, or abortion, or genetic engineering, or artificial human 'enhancement', or extreme cosmetic surgery, or transgender surgery, is ipso facto unreasonable? Even if opposition to any one of these is in fact unreasonable, this cannot be demonstrated at the drop of a hat. It requires philosophical argumentation, sometimes quite abstruse, to get to the heart of such issues. Reasonable people disagree, both within the academy and outside it. There is a long tradition of heated debate, popular and scholarly, over what we might label conservative and permissive views in medical ethics. Yet reasonable disagreement, and the correlative protection of basic freedoms that should follow from it in a liberal, professedly tolerant society, seems rapidly to be descending the ladder of priorities for people who call themselves liberal.

Freedom of religion is certainly on the back foot across Western society. When a baker can be found guilty of discrimination simply for refusing to decorate a cake with a pro-'gay marriage' slogan (about which more later),[4] when a city council can try to prevent a small Orthodox Jewish synagogue from meeting to pray in a private home,[5] and

---

4 https://www.theguardian.com/uk-news/2016/oct/24/born-again -christian-ashers-bakery-lose-court-appeal-in-gay-cake-row [last accessed 20.10.17].

5 http://www1.cbn.com/cbnnews/us/2015/June/Toras-Chaim-Synagogue [last accessed 20.10.17].

when parents can be prevented from withdrawing their children from compulsory sex education that violates their religious or ethical beliefs,[6] one can be sure that religious believers are under pressure to go against their own deeply held beliefs in areas that only a few decades ago were off limits to state intervention.

What is the solution to this problem? How should freedom of conscience and religion be protected in a liberal society? The main theme of this book is that liberal societies need a developed statutory and case-law framework, built on sound legal and ethical theory, for freedom of conscience and religion to be given the sort of fundamental protection it deserves. Mere piecemeal protection afforded by various 'conscience clauses' is not sufficient; nor is the somewhat vague, skeletal protection offered by various treaties and conventions. Rather, overarching protection for freedom of conscience in a liberal society starts with a concept I am going to call *involvement*. Involvement means a citizen's being bound up, to a greater or lesser degree, in the affairs and transactions of others. We are all involved in the affairs and transactions of some other citizens, to some extent – with our family, friends, neighbours, fellow members of this or that organisation or body, with our co-religionists, members of the same ethnic or cultural group, and

---

6   As in some European countries such as Austria and Denmark: http://
www.publications.parliament.uk/pa/jt200910/jtselect/jtrights/57/5704
.htm, section 1.30; http://www.europarl.europa.eu/RegData/etudes/note/
join/2013/462515/IPOL-FEMM_NT(2013)462515_EN.pdf, p. 12
[last accessed 20.10.17].

our compatriots.[7] But how far does this go? More precisely, how far *should* it go?

My case study for this monograph will be health care, where issues of freedom of religion and conscience are most prominent. I will argue that a developed legal and policy framework can provide the protection that conscientious objectors lack, but that certain theoretical mistakes need to be avoided in order for the framework to be feasible. Surprisingly, perhaps, I will appeal in part to a sophisticated tradition in Catholic moral theology where issues concerning the 'ethics of cooperation' have been worked out in detail. The theory from that tradition offers a way in which conscientious objectors can avoid the kind of involvement in health-care activities to which they object. But it also draws various distinctions that allow certain kinds of involvement, on ethical grounds, that should not trouble the conscience of a reasonable objector. Focusing mainly on the UK and the US, I will argue that the courts should incorporate a 'jurisprudence of cooperation' into their decision-making. This would give conscientious objectors a well-founded legal protection that they currently lack. Were it to be supplemented by substantial statutory protection, freedom of conscience and religion would be put on a much sounder footing than it is now.

Although my main concern is health care, I will also expand the discussion to some broader, deeper and even

---

7   Some will want to extend the 'circle of involvement' beyond a nation's boundaries. There is such involvement, of course, but its extent is a controversial matter. For my purposes, though, it is enough to stay within the borders of one's own country.

more vexed issues surrounding the concept of involvement. Freedom of conscience and religion in a liberal society, I argue, derives at least partly from an even more basic freedom – *freedom of association*. Whom we associate with, our choice of friends, partners, business associates, neighbours, and so on, is a matter of our *free choice*. Freedom of contract, on which our hallowed law of contract is built, itself presupposes freedom of association. Without freedom of association, there cannot even be a liberal society. Freedom of association is one of the first things that totalitarian regimes all but abolish. It may be that the attacks on freedom of religion will only increase. A jurisprudence of cooperation may well offer protection in certain areas, such as health care; but what if a conscientious objector refuses even to be *involved* in certain activities or institutions they believe to be an affront to their religious or ethical values? What if we reach a stage where liberal societies no longer merit the name 'liberal' but become what we might call 'secular authoritarian'? Needless to say, by that stage it will be too late to protect freedom of religion. That is why something needs to be done *now*, while liberalism is still adhered to by most of our elected officials and judicial appointees, in order to enshrine protections that one day may become unavailable. My suggestions will be tentative, to say the least. Still, I will raise the question of whether we need to recognise freedom of *dissociation*, a necessary corollary of freedom of association, as a fundamental right. In other words, might policymakers find a way of recognising a right *not to be involved* in something that a person or group objects to on grounds of conscience? Could legislation give voice to a basic freedom either to *abstain* from involvement, or *withdraw* from involvement, on conscientious grounds? This might seem like an extreme suggestion – maybe it is – but it may also be that the threat to freedom of religion is now so great that extreme suggestions must be entertained. At least a public discussion might begin on whether freedom of dissociation has the potential to resolve the increasing conflict between religion and secularism in liberal societies.

Overview of topics covered

I begin, in chapter 2, with a survey of some important examples of attacks on freedom of conscience, mainly but not exclusively from within health care. At the time of writing, the fate of President Obama's Affordable Care Act 2010 ('Obamacare') looks bleak given the presidency of Donald Trump. Nevertheless, the Act introduced some important 'mandates' for health insurance that have had a serious impact on freedom of conscience in the US, with important cases and ongoing litigation as a result. I will outline the American situation and raise serious questions about the state of the law, to which I return later. In the UK, the freedom of conscience debate has been confined to relatively narrower grounds in health care, mainly surrounding abortion. I set out the well-known case of *Doogan and Wood* (2014), where the UK Supreme Court ruled against freedom of conscience. Later I will return to the case in some more detail, showing what might be done by common law and statute to afford greater protection. In this chapter I also note pressure on freedom of conscience in Canada with respect to euthanasia, the role of religious freedom in European Union law (since Brexit is a vexed issue for the UK), and the highly contentious question of freedom of conscience when it relates to such things as adoption by homosexual couples and 'gay marriage'.

Chapter 3 goes into the British and American legal situations in more detail. In the UK, freedom of conscience needs a microscope to be visible, at least when it comes to health care. There is no blanket protection as there is for many other rights,[8] especially those of favoured groups such as women, the disabled, ethnic minorities and gays. Piecemeal protection is found here and there, with some vague, general treaty coverage and statutory lip service – but conscientious objectors cannot find the sort of legal shelter they merit. The US has a much stronger system of protection, but it has become mired in controversy lately in the wake of the Obamacare mandates. Overall, the law in the UK and the US is not nearly what it should be. In the US there has been some questionable judicial reasoning emanating from the Supreme Court. In the UK, the legislative protection for freedom of conscience is so narrow that the courts have very little room for manoeuvre.

How can we escape this mess if we are to accord freedom of religion and freedom of conscience the protection they deserve in a liberal society? A good start can be made by asking the courts to take judicial notice of work already done by philosophers on what I call the 'ethics of

---

8 Despite what is in the Equality Act 2010, about which more later.

cooperation in wrongdoing'. The US Supreme Court, in the famous *Hobby Lobby* judgment of 2014, took notice of my own research in the area. My work drew on a tradition of Catholic moral theology in which theologians – acting more as philosophers than as spokesmen for the Catholic religion – have developed a theory of the ethics of cooperation that is plausible in its own right and can be applied fruitfully to difficult cases. The theory itself has nothing particularly religious about it: it stands as a piece of moral philosophy. In chapter 4 I outline the theory, showing how it can deal with tricky cases where freedom of conscience or religion is at issue. If incorporated into the law, judges would be able to provide much broader and principled (rather than ad hoc) protection for these fundamental freedoms.

Chapter 5 delves more deeply into some of the important case law. I argue that the US Supreme Court in *Hobby Lobby* may have decided the case correctly but they did not do so for the right reasons. The court's rationale, relying on a 'mere sincerity' test of cooperation, produced a result that secured the plaintiff's freedom of conscience, but at the price of potentially generating absurd results in the future. The mistaken use of a mere sincerity test might in fact backfire on defenders of religious freedom, producing a judicial and government backlash that undermined this freedom even more. In the case of *Zubik v. Burwell*, I argue, we already see some of the absurd implications of a mere sincerity test playing out.

In the UK, the Supreme Court case of *Doogan and Wood* went against the conscientious objectors to abortion, but here the decision probably could not have gone any other way given the highly limited protection afforded to freedom of religion. Once again, adopting a jurisprudence of cooperation based on sound philosophical principles would have allowed the court some flexibility in judging whether the plaintiffs in this case were being asked to do something that made them objectively illicit cooperators in actions contrary to their deeply held religious and ethical beliefs.

I then consider the state of equality law in the UK in the light of the recent Equality Act and accompanying regulations. The UK now gives blanket statutory protection to a long list of 'protected characteristics' including 'religion or belief'. But do all these characteristics get *equal* protection? I argue that, at least as far as 'religion or belief' is concerned, UK equality law is a charter for inequality. It forces religious believers into situations and activities that violate their deeply held beliefs. Again, putting freedom of religion and conscience on a sounder common law and legislative footing would, as they say, 'level the playing field'.

How far, though, can freedom of conscience go? In chapter 6 I explore some broader and deeper issues about the extent to which, in a liberal society, freedom of conscience should be protected. We live in a pluralistic, multicultural, liberal, democratic, largely secular society in which there is constant competition by various groups for respect of their rights by government and the law. If a recent survey is to be believed, only 30 per cent of UK citizens consider themselves 'religious',[9] and although the figure is much

---

9   http://cde.peru21.pe/doc/0/0/2/9/4/294004.pdf [last accessed 29.4.18].

higher in the US, note that religiosity varies significantly by state, with left-liberal states such as New York and California registering much lower religiosity (similar to the UK) than more conservative states such as those in the South.[10] Unsurprisingly, one sees more reports of religious-secular tension in the former than in the latter, although even in conservative states conflicts arise.

How then, looking at the situation more broadly, should freedom of conscience be protected? Note that I do not say 'could': in a liberal society it is not a question of *whether* to protect freedom of conscience but *how*. Case-by-case, piecemeal approaches are bound to lead to problems and general 'drag' when it comes to protecting a fundamental right in a liberal society. It is a reactive rather than a proactive strategy: conscientious objectors will need constantly to justify themselves in each individual area of social life in which they find themselves under threat, pressuring legislators, or the courts in specific cases, to take their rights seriously enough to carve out this or that isolated accommodation. A piecemeal approach is of necessity haphazard, subject to the 'hot-button' issues of the moment, whereas the issues that no one is talking about are ignored. One might object that they will be ignored because conscience will not in such areas be under threat. This is an overly rosy way of looking at it. An area might be ignored not because it is safe for conscientious objection but because no one but those directly affected happens to be interested in it

---

10 https://en.wikipedia.org/wiki/List_of_U.S._states_by_religiosity [last accessed 20.10.17].

at the time. Why should a conscientious objector wait for the wider public, the courts or the legislature to take an interest before consideration is given to protecting them?

More generally, and more importantly, the enshrining of freedom of religion and conscience, in the substantive way I will defend, means the formulation of rules that act as a disincentive to those who would otherwise seek to violate the freedom. Further, broad principles provide overarching guidance. They structure the interpretation and evaluation of individual cases. A piecemeal approach can appeal to no general structure and rules of protection. Common law is famed for its development of case law in light of the peculiarities of individual cases, to be sure; but the aim is always for the development to result in general principles that are of value as judicial precedent. When it comes to fundamental rights, the general provisions found in statute and case law combine to form the strongest protective framework. Either can work on its own; they work best together. Piecemeal 'carve-outs' for fundamental rights, however, are insufficient. We expect more than this for other basic rights – so why should freedom of religion and conscience be any different?

Perhaps, for some, a broader-brush approach would be more satisfying. Here I will develop, briefly, the idea of 'freedom of dissociation' – the thought that just as freedom of association is a fundamental right in a free society (a civil right, recognised by the state), so should its converse be recognised. Freedom of dissociation is the right *not* to associate, or to *withdraw* from association, with other individuals or groups. The terminology of 'dissociation' or ('disassociation') might evoke in some readers thoughts of 'secessionism' or 'balkanisation', as though freedom of dissociation, at least as I am explaining it, entailed the total break-up of a society, or its sharp disintegration into factionalism. Yet it is hard to see why such results inevitably follow any more than that freedom of association leads to extreme social cohesion. The right to associate hardly means that everyone in a society will join the same group or groups (apart from belonging to the society itself). Similarly, the right to dissociate hardly implies that everyone will withdraw or disengage willy-nilly, or in huge swathes, from the bulk of social activities. Moreover, the right to dissociate should be seen as not being *essentially* a group right. Individuals should have freedom of dissociation as much as freedom of association. Even within relatively homogeneous social groups some members will choose to dissociate, whether on grounds of conscience, pure preference or something in between, from activities to which other members of the same groups will have no objection.

Secessionism, balkanisation and similar quasi-apocalyptic ideas (at least in the eyes of some political theorists) are essentially group concepts, and they generally have geopolitical or interstate ramifications. They affect entire states, and as movements they can have motivations that are far removed from what usually moves individuals and groups seeking *selective* dissociation *within* a society. Secessionism is usually about large-scale oppression, or a longstanding lack of political integration, or major economic grievances, and so on. Selective dissociation, at least of the kind I have in mind as an admittedly tentative way of grounding freedom of conscience and religion, is of a different degree altogether from balkanisation, and usually of a different kind. The former might morph into the latter in extreme situations, but extreme situations should, so to speak, not make the conceptual running.

Freedom of association is, I would argue, the moral basis of key elements of freedom of contract: I may transact with whom I like, for any purpose that is not harmful to individuals or society in general. It is also plausibly seen as the basis of core aspects of property rights: if I am not free to prohibit your entry to my property, or for that matter to send you away once you have entered it, my property rights amount to nothing. Without property rights and freedom of contract, a society cannot be called free. There is, of course, more to freedom of contract and property rights than freedom of association; but if you take away the latter, all the other elements of contract and property rights become either meaningless or futile.

I propose, then, that freedom of dissociation, as the converse of freedom of association, is a key moral right that could undergird freedom of religion and conscience in a society such as ours. Given its wide societal ramifications, it is the sort of moral right that deserves legal protection as a basic *civil* right – a right that belongs to citizens by virtue of their citizenship. This is already the case with freedom of association: no one can be coerced by the state into, say, joining a trade union or a political party, or becoming a member of this or that advocacy group. Similarly, citizens should be protected from the state's coercing them into being *involved* or *engaged* with other individuals or groups if they do not want to. Freedom of dissociation will then apply, ipso facto, both to individuals and to groups whose members wish to protect themselves from coercion in matters of conscience.

Yet we are immediately faced with the worry that freedom of dissociation could be appealed to in defence of various forms of prejudice and unjustified discrimination. Why couldn't a person or group use their freedom of dissociation to exclude others for no good reason, or to give concrete form to prejudices, whether religious, ethnic, racial, cultural, and so on, that liberal societies consider part of a less enlightened past? Why couldn't freedom of conscience be used positively to harm others in ways no society should tolerate? I will explore these sensitive issues, suggesting ways in which freedom of dissociation should and should not be understood so as to deflect these wholly justified concerns about its possible abuse.

Finally, in chapter 7, I propose concrete ways in which UK policymakers can give protection to freedom of religion and conscience in a way that does not derogate from the rights of anyone else. I suggest that Parliament follow the lead of the US by enacting something like the Religious Freedom Restoration Act 1993, which gives solid statutory protection against 'substantial burdens' on freedom of religion. It should incorporate freedom of conscience generally, and it should apply both to individuals and groups (such as corporations and other private bodies, whether or not directly recognised in law). When it comes to case law the courts should, when interpreting and implementing the legislation, not rely on a 'mere sincerity' test of religious belief. They should, for example, take judicial notice of a worked-out 'ethics of cooperation' whereby they are able to determine, on objective grounds, whether a group or individual makes a reasonable protest against behaviour that violates their sincere and deeply held beliefs. In other words, there needs to be a common-law block against abuse of freedom of conscience in cases where the objector may reasonably cooperate with some requirement that conflicts with their beliefs.

2   THE ATTACK ON FREEDOM OF CONSCIENCE

The Obamacare mandate

At the time of writing, during the presidency of Donald Trump, President Barack Obama's Affordable Care Act 2010, otherwise known as 'Obamacare', looks to have an uncertain future at best. Nevertheless, this legislation – extending taxpayer-funded health insurance to millions of Americans – brought with it a serious threat to religious freedom. Government regulations under the Act required employers to include in their coverage various forms of contraception (including abortifacient) unless the employer was a church. Many politicians and religious bodies protested at what they saw as a direct attack on religious freedom and freedom of conscience.[1] A Senate amendment that would have allowed employers to refuse to include contraception in health-care coverage if it was 'contrary

---

1   See, for instance, the United States Conference of Catholic Bishops (http://www.usccb.org/issues-and-action/religious-liberty/our-first-most-cher ished-liberty.cfm), the Republican Party (https://www.pagop.org/2012/02/obamas-attack-on-religious-liberty/), the Heritage Foundation (http://www.askheritage.org/how-is-president-obama-attacking-religious-liber ty/) and many other individuals and organisations. [All pages last accessed 20.10.17.]

to [their] religious beliefs or moral convictions' was de-
feated. In response to the widespread outcry, the Obama
government introduced various 'opt-outs' for certain religious organisations. In 2014 a private, for-profit corporation challenged the mandate, going all the way to the US
Supreme Court. The Court found in favour of the corporation, holding that the religious freedom of its owners was
substantially burdened by having to provide coverage for
forms of contraception to which they objected on religious
and moral grounds (Burwell 2014). Since then, however,
various religious or semi-religious bodies have objected
to the very idea of opting out of the mandated coverage.
They think that opting out is itself a form of immoral cooperation in the provision of the coverage they object to,
since the government or another insurance company then
steps in to fill the gap. We will see that this has created
something of a legal quagmire in the US, one that could be
avoided by rethinking the issues at stake.

The Obamacare mandate controversy is a major example of attempted government compulsion of people to
act against their consciences in important moral matters. Whether or not we agree with the stance of the conscientious objectors on the particular issue – abortion or
contraception – we should be concerned that this sort of
compulsion not be present in a liberal society.

The UK midwives

In 2014 the UK Supreme Court also handed down an important judgment on freedom of conscience, again in the

area of health care and again – unsurprisingly – on the subject of abortion (Doogan 2014). Here, two Scottish midwives objected to what they believed to be participation in abortions, to which they were religiously and ethically opposed. They already had a statutory exemption to taking in part in the actual termination of pregnancy, under s.4 of the Abortion Act 1967. Subsection 1 provides that no person is under a duty 'to participate in any treatment authorised by this Act to which he has a conscientious objection' (Abortion Act 1967, s.4(1)). The petitioners were midwives in Scotland who believed that 'any involvement in the process of termination render[ed] them accomplices to and culpable for that grave offence' (Doogan 2014: 7). Since they had a statutory exemption to 'participation', they objected to 'delegating, supervising and/or supporting staff to participate in and provide care to patients throughout the termination process' (Doogan 2014: 9) on the grounds that these were all forms of participation.

The Supreme Court held against the midwives, however. The 'participation' to which the Abortion Act referred, said the Court, was the actual procedure of terminating pregnancy. Ancillary activities such as those to which the midwives were also opposed were not covered by statute and, as such, were not subject to an exemption on conscience grounds. Again, I submit, had there been a general protection of freedom of conscience, rather than a particular conscience clause concerning one specific type of activity, the midwife petitioners would have stood a much greater chance of having their religious freedom protected. Moreover, had the Court been possessed of a worked-out jurisprudence covering cooperation in activities deemed immoral by an objector, they could have worked out reasonably well what sorts of activities might or might not be covered by the general statutory protection. The midwives might have succeeded, but with little risk of abuse of the protection.

Canadian euthanasia

Although my discussion will focus on the UK and US, it is interesting to consider other jurisdictions where freedom of religion and conscience is under threat. For example, in 2016 a Joint Committee on Physician-Assisted Dying reported to the Canadian Parliament on regulation of euthanasia (Ogilvie and Oliphant 2016). Professing that it 'respects a health care practitioner's freedom of conscience while at the same time respecting the needs of a patient who seeks medical assistance in dying,' the committee recommended that 'at a minimum' the practitioner should provide an 'effective referral' for the patient. Yet if the practitioner is *required to facilitate* euthanasia by means of a referral, it does not seem that their freedom of conscience is respected. As we will see, freedom of conscience extends beyond actual *participation* in an objectionable act and applies to certain types of assistance or *cooperation* as well.

The EU versus conscience

The European Union proclaims in various official documents the right to freedom of conscience and religion.

Article 9 of the European Convention on Human Rights recognises 'freedom of thought, conscience and religion', including freedom 'to manifest [one's] religion or belief, in worship, teaching, practice and observance'. The freedom is 'subject only to such limitations as are prescribed by law and are necessary in a democratic society in the interests of public safety, for the protection of public order, health or morals, or for the protection of the rights and freedoms of others.' In 2013 the European Council produced a detailed set of guidelines (European Council 2013) in which it cites as foundation for EU law in this matter the Universal Declaration of Human Rights (Article 18) and the International Covenant on Civil and Political Rights (Article 18), which give voice to freedom of religion and conscience in similar fashion. These guidelines 'on the promotion and protection of freedom of religion or belief' state that the limitations 'must be strictly interpreted'. Moreover, 'religion' and 'belief' are to be 'broadly construed'; and freedom to manifest these 'encompasses a broad range of acts'.

Nevertheless, EU jurisprudence is rather mixed on freedom of conscience and religion, and does not appear to be overly friendly to it. The European Committee of Social Rights recently declared that the European Social Charter 'does not impose on states a positive obligation to provide a right to conscientious objection for health care workers' (FAFCE 2013: 16). Sweden's strong protection for abortion rights, disallowing conscientious refusal of abortion services, was defended by the Committee. The European Court of Human Rights has decided that no pharmacist can refuse to sell legal contraceptives due to religious or conscientious objection (Pichon 2001). Yet the European Court has also said on occasion that where a state does allow conscientious refusal by a person to provide some legally available service, it should ensure that the person asking for the service can obtain it elsewhere (Poland 2011: sec. 206). As I will argue, this latter approach, if implemented fairly and properly, would give far greater protection to freedom of conscience and religion than a restrictive interpretation that effectively allowed other rights to 'trump' this freedom.

Weddings, adoptions, holidays, operations

The focus of this monograph is on health care, but clearly there are broader issues that need to be addressed, however controversial they may be. For example, recent cases in the US and UK have been hostile to people objecting on religious grounds to certain actions they believe support or assist in the promotion of homosexuality. At the time of writing, a Colorado baker has appealed to the US Supreme Court against a finding of discrimination by a state court due to his refusal in conscience to bake a wedding cake for a gay couple.[2] In the UK, a Belfast baker has appealed to the UK Supreme Court in a similar case: the baker refused to sell to a gay man a cake with a message on it saying 'Support Gay Marriage', and was found guilty of discrimination by a lower court (Ashers 2016). The UK Supreme Court

---

2   http://www.scotusblog.com/case-files/cases/masterpiece-cakeshop-ltd
    -v-colorado-civil-rights-commn/ [last accessed 05.05.18].

recently held that the owners of a Christian guest house were guilty of discrimination for not renting a room to a gay couple in a 'civil partnership' (Bull 2013). Also in the UK, a number of Catholic charities have shut down their adoption services rather than face penalties for refusing to allow adoption by homosexual couples; others have chosen to remove the word 'Catholic' from their names.[3] The same has happened in the US.[4] And at the time of writing, an American woman seeking transgender surgery has sued a Catholic hospital for refusing to perform a hysterectomy as part of the process.[5] Though the final legal outcome of some of these cases is undetermined at the time of writing, the trend is clear; and it is evident we will see more such cases in future.

We have to ask ourselves some hard questions about how, in a liberal, pluralistic society, with many diverse ethical and religious (as well as non-religious) viewpoints, where there is so much fundamental disagreement about basic ideas of right and wrong, the rights of everyone can be accommodated. These questions go to the heart of what makes a society free in the first place. Freedom of contract and property rights, themselves closely connected to the basic freedom of association, are surely a *sine qua non* of a

3   http://www.catholicherald.co.uk/commentandblogs/2013/07/04/how -many-catholic-adoption-societies-have-actually-closed-down-and-how -many-are-now-quietly-handing-children-over-to-gay-adoptive-parents/ [last accessed 20.10.17].

4   http://www.catholic.org/news/national/story.php?id=41680 [last accessed 20.10.17].

5   http://www.catholicherald.co.uk/news/2017/01/06/catholic-hospital-sued -for-refusing-to-carry-out-sex-change-procedure/ [last accessed 20.10.17].

free society. Whom we do business with, whom we choose as our friends, partners, associates, our freedoms as members of families and other groups – these all go to make up the foundations of a society that any reasonable person would recognise as free and 'liberal' with a very small 'l'.

At the same time, however, our liberal society contains many laws and regulations governing various types of discrimination – the unfair favouring or disfavouring of one person or group over another because of a characteristic our society deems to be irrelevant to how people should be treated. Here, unsurprisingly, there are basic disagreements between people and groups over which characteristics are relevant to how people are treated. The vast majority of people consider mere skin colour to be irrelevant: treating someone differently merely because of their skin colour rightly strikes many of us as unacceptable. The same goes for gender. What about ethnic origin? Not giving someone a job merely because of where they come from also seems wholly unreasonable. It is, however, legal in the UK to set up a club for members of one gender or people of one ethnic origin and to exclude from membership anybody else.[6] The same goes for religious clubs, yet at the same time refusing to serve someone in a restaurant because, say, they are Hindu or Muslim is illegal.

A brief perusal of the laws and regulations governing discrimination and equal treatment in the UK reveals, in

---

6 Equality (2010). See, for explanation, p. 20 of the Equality and Human Rights Commission document at https://www.equalityhumanrights.com/sites/default/files/what_equality_law_means_for_your_association2c_club_or_society.pdf [last accessed 20.10.17].

my view, as much confusion as clarity. To be frank, the law is a bit of a mess, with not even the experts knowing how certain cases stand until they are tested in court (which may never happen). To a certain extent this is a strength of our common law system, where judges build incrementally on previous decisions in light of complex factual circumstances. Still, when the principles governing particular cases are themselves unclear we have serious weakness in the system and the potential for abuse or arbitrariness.

What we see in the cases I have outlined above is that governments and courts have not allowed conscientious objectors to opt out of providing services that go against their deeply held moral or religious convictions, even though the same services were freely available from other providers. To put it another way, conscientious objectors have been compelled to be 'involved' or 'implicated' in that to which they object, on pain of being found guilty of discrimination or of somehow preventing the exercise by other individuals and groups of their rights and freedoms under the law. It is not clear that this is an acceptable state of affairs in a genuinely liberal and pluralistic society, nor that freedom of religion and conscience can receive adequate protection when conscientious objectors face such restrictions on their behaviour.

3　THE STATE OF THE LAW: UNCLEAR AND INADEQUATE

UK: freedom of conscience needs a microscope

Leaving broader issues aside for now, when it comes to freedom of conscience *just in health care*, an area where conscience issues perhaps loom largest of all, you need a microscope to see it at work in the UK. The proof is this: supporters of conscience rights in *abortion alone* are still seriously concerned that this freedom is not being given adequate protection (All Party 2016). If, fifty years after the legalisation of abortion, there is ongoing debate about the rights of conscience despite there being a form of conscience protection in the Abortion Act 1967 itself, then the situation outside the abortion area cannot be much better.

The Abortion Act contains a 'conscience clause' to the effect that no one with a 'conscientious objection' is under a duty to 'participate in any treatment' authorised by the Act. Yet there is a sweeping exception immediately following, preventing the clause from applying where the treatment is 'necessary to save the life or to prevent grave permanent injury to the physical or mental health of a pregnant woman' (Abortion 1967). Now, as we have already seen, the UK Supreme Court has made it clear that 'treatment' refers only to the process of termination of pregnancy itself, from beginning to end – not to any ancillary activities such as managing an abortion ward or booking women in for abortions (Doogan 2014). So unless a doctor, or midwife, or other health-care employee, can reach a voluntary arrangement with their manager to avoid activities such as these to which they might object on conscience grounds, there is no protection.

Outside the fraught area of abortion, the only other conscience clause protecting health-care workers in the UK concerns human embryo experimentation and *in vitro* fertilisation procedures (HFEA 1990: [s.38]). This means that a person who objects to depriving a comatose patient of food and water,[1] or to being involved in the provision of transgender surgery, or extreme cosmetic surgery, or contraceptives (perhaps to an adolescent), or to giving sexual counselling to homosexual couples,[2] or to doing anything that contravenes their deeply held and sincere ethical or religious beliefs, has no quarter. This is so *however freely the services objected to may be available from other parties or sources* – a crucial feature to which I will return at some length.

---

1   Removal of 'artificial nutrition and hydration', which has been legal since the House of Lords judgment in Bland (1993).

2   As happened in McFarlane (2010), where a counsellor who so objected was denied appeal, the decision being upheld by the European Court of Human Rights.

Although, at the time of writing, the UK is in the process of exiting the EU, it is highly likely that the nominal conscience and religious freedom protection afforded under the European Convention on Human Rights will continue in some form. Perhaps the Human Rights Act 1998, which currently enshrines the ECHR (European Convention on Human Rights) protections in domestic law, will be replaced. It is unthinkable, however, that Article 9 of the ECHR, or a close relative, will not continue in force. The question is: will it be seriously enforced? The think tank ResPublica has expressed dismay at the current paucity of protection for freedom of religion and conscience in UK law (Orr 2016). It decries the 'the relentless privatisation of religious beliefs and the exclusion of religion from public life', proposing that there be a 'reasonable accommodation' clause in any future human rights legislation that would give conscientious objectors, whether in health care or beyond, freedom not to be involved in acts or practices contrary to their deeply held beliefs.

Interestingly, Lady Hale, Deputy President of the Supreme Court, has used the very same language of 'reasonable accommodation' to express her own concerns that a 'fair balance' has yet to be struck between competing individual rights, and also between individual rights and those of the community (Hale 2014). It was Lady Hale who gave the Court's judgment in *Doogan and Wood* that the midwives had no protection from being required to carry out various abortion-related actions that violated their religious and ethical beliefs. Again, Lady Hale agreed with the Court in *Bull v. Hall* that the Christian guest house owners wrongfully discriminated against a homosexual couple by not renting them a room. In her view, however, it may well be that a 'conscience clause' for employees or for providers of goods and services is needed for the hoped-for 'reasonable accommodation' to be realised.

The US: the battle of the courts since *Hobby Lobby*

The US has historically provided much stronger protection to freedom of religion and conscience given the First Amendment to the Constitution, under which 'Congress shall make no law respecting an establishment of religion, or prohibiting the free exercise thereof'. Interestingly, early drafts of this part of the amendment explicitly mentioned 'conscience' as well as 'religion', but the former term did not make it to the final text.[3] Yet the legal and jurisprudential tradition is clear that freedom of conscience, broadly construed, is covered by the First Amendment.[4]

Federal legislation has bolstered this basic protection, notably with the Religious Freedom Restoration Act 1993 (RFRA 1993). The Act prohibits the federal government from 'substantially burdening' a person's 'exercise of religion' unless a stringent test (called 'strict scrutiny') is

---

3   See http://www.religioustolerance.org/amend_1.htm [last accessed 20.10.17].

4   For a leading case supporting non-religious conscientious objection to military service, see the US Supreme Court in Welsh (1970).

satisfied. First, the proposed law under scrutiny must be 'demonstrated by the government' to serve a 'compelling governmental interest'. Secondly, it must be shown to be 'the least restrictive means of furthering that compelling governmental interest'. In other words, the substantial burden will not stand if the government has a less burdensome – perhaps totally non-burdensome – way of furthering its *compelling* interest in having such a law.

The test is deliberately strict, formulated in response to a weakening in the 1980s of religious freedom by means of 'generally applicable' laws that did not target specific religions (for instance a ban on drugs as opposed to a ban on particular drugs used in a particular religious tradition, such as that of some American Indians). The most famous test of RFRA thus far has been the *Hobby Lobby* case (Burwell 2014), where the Supreme Court held that a for-profit corporation was not subject to the Obamacare 'contraceptive mandate'. This federal mandate requires[5] employers to provide their workers with health insurance coverage including for contraceptives. Although exemptions were already explicitly made for religious organisations such as churches, for-profit corporations were a key target of the mandate and so not exempted. The employers in *Hobby Lobby*, however, had religious and ethical objections to abortifacient contraceptive methods (that destroy the already-conceived embryo). They argued that their religious freedom was substantially burdened by

---

5   Although at the time of writing the mandate is still on the books, it has been substantially weakened by President Trump and is likely to be abolished.

the mandate since their company, which was a 'closely held' family enterprise,[6] would be effectively shut down by the enormous financial penalties imposed by the government for non-compliance.

The Supreme Court agreed. Even a closely held for-profit corporation could claim protection under the RFRA. This was a significant extension of freedom of religion and conscience, but it has also generated yet more litigation. Even if the current mandate does not survive, it is likely that new laws, either at state or federal level, will force recourse to the RFRA by litigants. The aftermath of *Hobby Lobby* has seen further challenges to the mandate and much confusion. A number of cases, particularly the ones consolidated into the Supreme Court case of *Zubik v. Burwell,* challenged the very accommodation that the court gave the plaintiffs in *Hobby Lobby* (Zubik 2016). Without deciding the merits, the Supreme Court vacated the previous appellate judgments that went against the plaintiff organisations and sent the case back down, where it remains at the time of writing. Later, I will outline why I think the Supreme Court itself is partly responsible for the confusion and what might be done to dispel it. Indeed, the confusion extends to the views of the most recent appointee to the Supreme Court to fill the vacant post left by the death of Antonin Scalia, the federal judge Neil Gorsuch.

---

6   Hence tying the company closely to the beliefs and character of its owners. This was a critical matter in the case, but is not relevant for present purposes.

The law is a mess

It is fair to say that the law relating to freedom of religion and conscience is a mess in both the UK and US – the focus of my discussion. In the UK there is little more than nominal protection under various conventions, as noted above; but we have seen that in practice this does not lead to much protection at all. Perhaps, then, the courts should simply be more active in enforcing provisions such as Article 9 of the ECHR, Article 18 of the International Covenant on Civil and Political Rights and Article 18 of the Universal Declaration of Human Rights, to which the UK is a signatory? True, such provisions have hardly loomed large in the sorts of cases I have mentioned, but more importantly the question is not *whether* to be more active, but *how*. Merely to require that these provisions be enforced does not tell us how this should be done. What, concretely, should be done to give extra protection to these freedoms? Although I will not be able to cover the field, I will make practical proposals for health care and, albeit more tentatively, for society broadly speaking.

For the moment, I observe simply that in the UK there is a single, narrow conscience clause exempting a conscientious objector from 'participating' in abortion, a similar non-participation conscience clause in respect of IVF and embryo research, some international conventions to which they UK is signatory and which provide abstract, general protection, and a Human Rights Act (implementing the ECHR) that, at the time of writing, is likely to be repealed in a few years and replaced by a new Bill of Rights or similar document. In addition, we have a jejune body of case law that demonstrates one thing only: if a conscientious objector is seeking protection, it will be largely a matter of luck whether they find themselves in front of a sympathetic judge, which is less likely to happen than not. If we compare this to the plethora of legislation, regulations and judicial pronouncements protecting people from discrimination on grounds of, say, gender, sexual orientation or disability, it would be difficult not to see those who seek to protect their religious freedom or freedom of conscience as being at a worrying disadvantage.

In the US, as I have indicated, things are a little more promising due to entrenched constitutional and legislative protections. The First Amendment is taken very seriously by most courts, by Congress and generally by the executive. The Religious Freedom Restoration Act gives freedom of religion and conscience broad and strong support. Given, however, the federal system of the US, and various court rulings, the federal RFRA only applies to the federal government. It does not apply to state and municipality law unless a state has passed its own version of the RFRA, which to date only 21 states have done.

Peculiarities of the US system aside, the central problem with the situation in America is, in a way, the reverse of what it is in the UK. Whereas, in the UK, protection is less than robust, in the US it is almost *too* robust. This might seem like a strange way of looking at it: given that my concern is to find ways of strengthening freedom of religion and conscience, why should I worry that the protection in America is overly strong? The problem, as we shall see, is that US courts have taken such a 'hands-off' approach to evaluating burdens on the rights of religion and conscience that it has led to a chaotic situation in the courts. Plaintiffs are trying to extricate themselves from situations in what I argue is an unreasonable way, and mistaken reasoning by the US Supreme Court has thrown lower court decisions into disarray. Judicial and statutory changes need to be made so that conscientious objectors have solid protection but not at the cost of a 'free for all' as to how widely the protection extends.

Participation is not enough

Let us return to the conscience clause embedded in the UK's Abortion Act. Section 4(1) says that 'no person shall be under any duty, whether by contract or by any statutory or other legal requirement, to participate in any treatment authorised by this Act to which he has a conscientious objection'. The section adds that the burden of proof is on the objector and that the protection does not extend to treatment necessary to 'save the life or to prevent grave permanent injury to the physical or mental health of a pregnant woman'.

The key word in this conscience clause is 'participation'. What does it mean? In ordinary parlance, by 'participate' we mean 'take part in' or, simply, 'do' an activity that other people are also doing, as in 'participate in a game of tennis' or 'participate in running the company'. Sometimes we mean something broader, but we usually qualify what we say to make this clear, as in 'participate in the event *as a spectator'*, since the *expectation* is that you are doing rather than merely watching. Normally it sounds odd even to make the qualification: we don't say 'I participated in the tennis match as a spectator'. So the very import of 'participate' is that you are *doing* that in which you participate. You are not a bystander, but you are also not a mere assistant or enabler of the conditions for the relevant act or behaviour to take place. Now I don't pretend that there are no fuzzy boundaries here or no exceptions to the rule, as there always are with language. But the core meaning of 'participate' is clear, and this is just how the UK Supreme Court interpreted the statutory term in *Doogan and Wood*.

Lady Hale – who, as we have seen, herself publicly laments the lack of protection for freedom of conscience in the UK – delivered the unanimous opinion of the court in holding that the Glasgow midwives had no statutory protection for any activities beyond actual participation in an abortion. She asserted: ' "Participate" in my view means taking part in a "hands-on" capacity' (Doogan 2014: 15). In other words, the conscience clause had to be interpreted narrowly, as Parliament intended, to cover only those activities that were *performative* in nature – part or whole of the acts that, together, end a pregnancy. This included such things as administration of medication before or after the abortion, as indicated by the procedure itself. It did not, however, include such activities as: taking calls to book abortions; managing shifts on the abortion ward; allocation of staff to patients; providing guidance and support to other midwives except when directly connected with a particular procedure for a particular patient; responding to calls for assistance except when specifically required as part of an abortion procedure; paging anaesthetists; providing support to family members (ibid.: 15–17).

In my view, given the law as it stands, the case was correctly decided, and for the right reasons: the ordinary sense of 'participate' is the sense adopted by the court, following what it deemed reasonably to be the intention of Parliament when it passed the Abortion Act. Nevertheless, we can see clearly what little protection the conscience clause afforded conscientious objectors such as the Glasgow midwives, for whom abortion was a deeply immoral act contrary to their religious and ethical beliefs. It was not *mere participation* to which the midwives objected, but other activities ancillary to the procedure itself that they held to *assist* or *facilitate* the provision of abortions. Such assistance or facilitation was, for them as for most conscientious objectors, deeply morally troublesome. We cannot accuse the midwives of having over-delicate consciences for not wanting to be involved in such things as booking abortions or managing shifts on the abortion ward. For such activities do indeed assist or facilitate the delivery of the procedures themselves.

It does not take much imagination to see how participation is not enough when it comes to sheltering individuals from actions to which they conscientiously object. Like most people, I would never participate in a burglary; but I would not hold the door of a victim's house open for a burglar either, unless my life or limb were in danger. Yet holding the door open is not, strictly, participation – at least if I didn't force it open in the first place but happened to be walking by when the burglar (improbably, I admit) called out for help. Nor would I give a thug the address of some innocent person I knew whom the thug wished to beat up: doing so would certainly trouble my conscience, even though it would not be participation in the beating itself.

In the next chapter I will say more about this. For now, the basic point is straightforward. If the government and the law are going to protect freedom of religion and conscience – as they must in any pluralistic, liberal democracy – then they have to do more than offer conscience clauses extending only as far as actual participation in some objectionable act. For such clauses provide very little protection given the complex network of action within which any specific deed takes place.

4   LAW NEEDS PHILOSOPHY: ETHICAL PRINCIPLES OF COOPERATION

How might you act wrongly? Let me count the ways

When we think of doing something wrong, we nearly always have mind what I call a 'primary act' – a particular wrong action such as stealing something, hurting an innocent person, murder, adultery, cheating on an exam, wilfully destroying someone else's property, and so on. But there are many other ways of acting wrongly *in relation to* the primary act, and we don't think of these much at all. Maybe if we did, to put it tweely, the world would be a better place.

You can act wrongly by, for example: *advising* someone to falsify their CV; *ordering* someone to commit a robbery; *agreeing* to shelter a wanted criminal from the police; being rude to someone and thereby *provoking* them to retaliate; *praising* an act of wanton cruelty; *hiding* evidence from the police; being *silent* when asked by your employer whether you have (and indeed you have) stolen office property; *defending* a person's act of rape.

These are all ways of being *implicated* in another person's (or your own) wrongful primary act. You *compound* the initial wrong done, by engaging in some further act or omission that may or may not be as bad as the primary act itself. It is strange that there is very little discussion of this in philosophy, law or even in ordinary life. Be that as it may, I have omitted the most serious way in which one can be implicated in a wrongful primary act without performing the act itself: this is by being an *assistant* or *cooperator* in that act. Being a cooperator is subsidiary to being a primary agent – the performer of the primary act – but it is a kind of *partnership* in that act that receives, as it were, some of its moral taint.

You can, of course, cooperate in perfectly permissible or even admirable acts – helping the proverbial old lady cross the road, assisting someone with the repair of their car – but these are not my concern here. My focus is wrongful behaviour, because this is where freedom of conscience and religion enter the scene. Most of us think that if an act is morally wrong, assisting someone to perform it is also morally wrong. Who doubts that rape is a serious wrong – and who would ever think it permissible to *help* someone commit a rape, say by holding down the victim? A conscientious objector to some act may want to avoid performing it, or they may want to avoid *cooperating* with it. If the wrongness of the act is something contained in or clearly entailed by their belief system, be it their religion or their code of ethics, the objector will rightly see any law requiring performance of or cooperation with the act as a serious restriction of one of their fundamental freedoms. This is at the root of all of the conscience cases that have, in increasing numbers over the last couple of decades, come before the courts.

In the UK, we see that conscientious objectors have very little real protection when it comes to the performance of actions to which they object; but when it comes to cooperation with such actions, the protection dwindles virtually to zero. The US offers much more protection, yet the courts there often go to the other extreme of giving sincerely held religious or ethical beliefs protection beyond all scrutiny. A balance needs to be struck, but it is not possible in the current legal framework. Neither case law nor statute in either country provides a way for conscientious objectors to obtain the protection they need and to an extent that does not end up being – as it might in America – counterproductive.

This is where philosophy comes in. We find philosophical reasoning throughout case law and also when legislators debate proposed statutes. Philosophical reasoning, especially on difficult and sometimes controversial ethical issues, is inescapable. It can be done well, or it can be done badly – superficially, without rigour, and in a tendentious way. But it has to be done, preferably with care and depth. Neither UK nor US law, nor their respective constitutional systems, could have the very character they have without the deep influence of thinkers going back to Plato and Aristotle, through medieval philosophers such as Aquinas, the empiricists such as Locke, Enlightenment natural law theorists, and the American Pragmatists. Law with philosophy might or might not become mere tyranny; but law without philosophy is *certain* to be tyranny, or else chaos. Neither judges nor legislators should fear philosophical influence on the development of law. Of course, they can ask – 'Which philosophy? Whose ideas? Do any two philosophers agree on anything?' The questions are all fair, but the only response a philosopher can make is to offer their ideas for inspection; it is up to others whether the ideas seem plausible enough to be worth incorporating into something wider. Moreover, if those ideas have some weight of history behind them, some kind of intellectual tradition, then at least they cannot be accused of having been conjured out of thin air.

Types of cooperation

Cooperation, as we have already seen, is a major ethical issue in many religious freedom cases, where conscientious objectors are individuals or organisations that cite religious principle or teaching as a reason for not cooperating with an act required by a particular law or regulation. We might expect, then, to find teaching on the ethics of cooperation in at least some religious teaching. I do not know of any such survey having been done, but certainly within the tradition of Catholic moral theology there is a well worked-out and robust teaching on cooperation. It is, I submit, reasonable and plausible *in its own right*, that is to say, independently of any specifically Catholic doctrine. To put it another way, it is a very good piece of straight moral philosophy or ethical theory, one that I have expounded and developed in several places. (For my previous work on the topic, see Oderberg (2003, 2017a,b).) If this sort of theory were made a standard part of judicial reasoning in conscience cases, we would find freedom of conscience and religion receiving much greater protection, but it would also place reasonable limits on that protection – thereby avoiding some of the excesses we currently find in the American courts.

I can only give a brief outline here, but at least sufficient to give the flavour of what a plausible ethics of cooperation looks like. The most important facet of the theory is that it makes many important distinctions between *kinds* of co-operation: it is not as though all cooperation is of a piece, to be morally evaluated in exactly the same way. For a start, there is the key distinction between *formal* and *material* cooperation. Formal cooperation involves a clear (explicit or maybe implicit) *intent* to share in the responsibility (or guilt) of the primary agent – the person whose initial act is the one with which cooperation can occur. If you assist someone to rob a bank with the *intention* that the bank be robbed, you are a formal cooperator. We should agree that this kind of purposive cooperation in wrongdoing is morally wrong and, when the primary act is criminal, it is usually an illegal act of aiding and abetting. Formal co-operation is not the sort of case that occupies the courts or concerns conscientious objectors. They object precisely because they do *not* intend for the wrongful act to take place; they are *unwilling* assistants. So our main concern is what is called *material* cooperation.

A material cooperator is in some way co-opted into as-sisting the primary agent, usually through physical duress or some lesser inducement. In criminal cases there is often the threat of violence ('Tell me the password or I'll blow your brains out'). In civil law, however, there is no threat of violence and conscience cases go well beyond what the criminal law usually regards as aiding and abetting. The duress is typically financial, for example: provide contraceptive health insurance or face a financial penalty, which may even involve loss of one's livelihood. There may be requirements to pay compensation, as in many anti-discrimination laws. The main point is that a material cooperator does not intend that the act he is cooperating with be performed, but he knows it (probably) will be if he cooperates.

How can a potential material cooperator decide whether it is morally permissible to cooperate? He needs to ask a number of questions about the nature of his cooperative act. One is whether his cooperative act is itself wrongful independently of the act with which he is cooperating. If helping someone cheat on an exam means bribing or threatening an examiner, then the cooperative act is itself intrinsically wrong. So the cooperative act has to be what we might call 'morally neutral' or 'indifferent'. Handing over one's own keys is itself indifferent, so is passing on public information. If either act assists another to enter a house for the purpose of theft, it can be impermissible material cooperation. A second question is whether the assistance is *mediate* or *immediate*. This is a subtle issue: what needs to be ascertained is whether the cooperator is *sharing* in the primary act *as if* they were an accomplice without being an accomplice. In other words, had the cooperator not been unwilling, would their act have been one of *joint participation*, whether in whole or in part, with the primary act? Helping someone carry away stolen goods is therefore immediate cooperation, whereas locating the target or driving the getaway car is mediate cooperation. Holding down the victim so the primary agent can rape her, even if it is done under pressure rather than willingly, is immediate cooperation. It is virtually as bad as carrying out the rape oneself, and would be condemned by most people.

We then come to more subtle questions concerning types of cooperation that are not of themselves morally wrong but might be so depending on the circumstances. Remember: the basic idea is that morality is about doing good and avoiding evil. No one, however, can avoid doing evil in all situations, short of sitting in an armchair and doing nothing at all. Life would grind to a halt if we were not morally permitted to do bad things, as long as they are not done *intentionally* and we have a *sufficiently good reason* for allowing those bad things to happen. Here we need first to classify, very generally, the kinds of situation a cooperator might find themselves in, and then evaluate their cooperation according to whether they have a good enough reason to cooperate *in that particular situation*.

Dispensability

One thing we need to ask is whether the cooperation is *dispensable or indispensable*. If the primary agent *depends* on another's cooperation it is indispensable, such as when someone supplies a homicidal weapon to another who cannot get it elsewhere. If the supplier is one of many available, then the cooperation of any one of them would be dispensable, in other words not causally necessary for the primary act. If you know the password to a bank account that the primary agent – a fraudster – wants to access and no one else but the absent owner does, your cooperation is indispensable, practically speaking. (Sure, the fraudster could try to crack the password using software, guesswork, and so on, but *practically* speaking these are all likely to be out of consideration.) If the password is freely available through an online leak, the fact that you've seen it makes your cooperation dispensable, assuming the primary agent knows he can find it by other means. Or suppose you are one of a number of people who know the password, all of whom are approachable by the fraudster. Or perhaps the password is known to be written down somewhere in the office, or stored unencrypted on the hard drive. In such cases you are a dispensable cooperator. It is not as though indispensable cooperation has to be an absolute *sine qua non* of the primary act, in the sense that without it the act simply cannot be performed short of a miracle. It is, rather, that the primary act, *practically speaking*, cannot be performed, or would be performed with great difficulty, or would have its probability significantly lowered without the cooperation. Providing the burglar with the code to a safe that only you know is as indispensable as can be, assuming no other means of access. Handing the burglar the keys to your car is dispensable, assuming the burglar could threaten anyone else to do the same with their car. As always, there is a spectrum of cases that could be considered.

Proximity

A further, very important question is whether the assistance is *proximate* or *remote*. This distinction concerns how far away the cooperative act is from the primary act, primarily but not solely in space and time. It is about how close the cooperator is, *causally speaking*, to the primary act itself. Put more loosely, the question is about how *implicated* or *caught up* in the primary act a cooperator is in terms of the latter's *causal role*. The question is one of where in the *causal chain* the cooperative act is relative to the main act – not an absolute matter, but relative to circumstances and alternative possibilities. Keeping it simple, we can see that selling petrol to a driver on the way to a burglary, even if the seller knows what the driver is up to, is quite remote. Giving specific directions to the house is more proximate. Showing the burglar where the key is hidden is very proximate. It is a question of what we might call 'executive character': is what the cooperator is doing so close, causally, to the primary act that it is a small step away from doing it themselves? Or, at the other extreme, is the cooperator so far removed from the main act that they are hardly more of an assistant than anyone else who is not involved at all? Between these extremes lies a broad spectrum, and it takes much subtlety of judgment and attention to detail – something at which judges are expert – to come to a reasonable conclusion about where a cooperator stands in the circumstances of the case.

Usually, a cooperator will be close in space and time to the primary act: handing over keys; providing a getaway vehicle; shredding documents – these sorts of cooperative act tend to take place close, in space and time, to the performance of the primary, wrongful act. But any of them could be done far in space and time from the main act, as could giving someone a password, providing equipment or signing a document. We can ask: how many key causal steps were there from the assistance to the primary act? The more steps involved, the more there is that can go wrong, or the more events can intervene to prevent the assistance from being *effective*. A bureaucrat who signs a minor administrative document, knowing that one of his senior managers is likely to use it to commit a fraud if the manager achieves various committee decisions in his favour, is quite remote as a cooperator. By contrast, a bureaucrat who shreds documents to help her immediate line manager cover up a fraud, with no further steps involved, is a highly proximate cooperator. In general, the closer a cooperator is, the more implicated they will be.

Again, handing over surgical instruments is more proximate than administering anaesthetic, which is more proximate than booking in a patient for surgery. Running the café that serves the coffee a surgeon needs to stay awake on the job is highly remote. We can see already that proximity judgments are not *absolute* – they are made *relative* to alternatives. This does not make such judgments purely subjective or a matter of opinion, any more than judging Fred to be taller than Barney is merely a matter of opinion even though the judgment that Fred is tall (with no further qualification) can never be absolutely true.

In other words, proximity judgments are implicitly *comparative*. Certain kinds of cooperation tend to be more proximate than others in most situations, but there are always fine judgments to be made. Booking a patient in for surgery might depend for its proximity on what else needs to happen before the surgery takes place. Nurse Wilma might object on conscience grounds to booking a woman in for an abortion where the booking is highly provisional, has to go through several steps of an approval process, where the risk of cancellation is very high, and so on. Nurse Betty might object to booking a woman for an abortion where, if she books her in, it is pretty certain that the booking will not change and the abortion will take place. Betty, *all other things being equal*, is a more proximate cooperator than Wilma, and *also* a proximate cooperator in the circumstances.

Having looked at some of the main ways we can classify acts of cooperation, the issue now is how to evaluate them morally. Here, we have to look at the *reasons* a cooperator might have for doing what they do.

Balancing goods and bads

What we ultimately want to know is how 'implicated' a given cooperator is *morally speaking*, not just how implicated they are as a matter of fact, in terms of proximity, dispensability, immediacy, and so on. The idea of implication that we want to home in on has a moral colour to it. It is not just about how close a person is, practically speaking, as a cooperator in a primary act. It is also about how implicated they are in terms of taking on some of the *moral responsibility* for that primary act. Here, we need to bring in the question of what *reasons* the cooperator might have for assisting the primary agent, and whether those reasons are *sufficient to justify* the particular kind of cooperation they perform.

We have to ask, first: how 'tightly connected' is the cooperator to the primary act in terms of causal factors, space and time, dispensability, executive character? At one end of the spectrum there are cooperative acts that are highly proximate, practically indispensable, perhaps even of such a character that it is virtually inconceivable that the primary agent could have achieved her objective without that specific form of assistance. At the other end we have acts that are very remote, highly dispensable, having the character of almost trivial, passing assistance. Contrast, say, giving the fraudster the unique password that only you know and that is the *only* way to access the bank account, with telling someone where they can take a class on computer science in a situation where you suspect they *might* use the information to learn how to gain unlawful access to a computer. These are obvious extremes; typical cases lie along a spectrum in between.

Our second question is: how do we balance the badness of the act with which the person is cooperating against the bad outcome that they are seeking to *avoid* by cooperating? To reiterate, a material cooperator is an *unwilling* assistant. He is pressured into helping the primary agent commit a wrongful act. This will be because of some incentive or inducement: by cooperating, the assistant avoids something bad happening to *him*. (Note that this might involve a threat to harm a third party such as a family member or loved one.)

Recall that the whole point of raising cooperation as an issue for conscientious objectors is that by cooperating in a bad act a person does a *further* bad act; and we should all minimise the number of bad acts we perform. But virtually everything we do has *some* bad result: every time we drive we contribute to pollution; every time we eat we add to waste; when we buy our mobile phones, we add just that little bit more support to some exploitative labour practice somewhere in the world. The only sure way to do no bad is to do *nothing at all* – and even that might plausibly be thought to be doing bad by *omitting* to do good!

We need, therefore, reasonable principles to allow us to go about our lives without the unhealthy and counter-product-ive scrupulosity of worrying that every little action coop-erates with some bad act somewhere in the world. On the other hand, there are limits: sometimes our acts are just *too close* to other bad acts to be 'off the hook', as it were, without sufficient justification. This is precisely the conscientious objector's healthy, albeit difficult, worry. So here are some very general principles that help us to evaluate cooperation cases, with the strong proviso that the devil is always in the details.

Before setting out these principles, though, note that for conscientious objection cases the first consideration is whether the objector *sincerely believes* the primary act, concerning which cooperation is an issue, is wrong on religious or broadly ethical grounds. In setting out the theory of cooperation I have, to avoid distraction, stuck to examples of acts, such as fraud and theft, on whose wrong-ness everyone agrees. In conscientious objection cases, ex hypothesi, there is no such agreement. The objector finds themselves at odds with the opinions of their colleagues or the wider public. Their moral or religious beliefs may in fact be wrong or at least unreasonable. When it comes to freedom of religion and conscience, however, the courts in liberal societies do not usually look behind the beliefs to their justification, let alone their truth. They are only concerned with whether the objector is a genuine believer in a genuine ethical or religious code. (Scientology rarely counts; Jedi never.) There may yet be cases in which no reasonable person could disagree that the particular conscientious objection at hand was unjustified – but to discuss this would take us well beyond the scope of the present discussion. Here, I argue, the rules of cooperation are subject to the test of reasonableness, whatever we may say about the primary acts with which they are connected. With this all-important caveat in place, we can now get an idea of how the rules operate.

Formal cooperation, as I have already suggested, is morally off limits. The same goes for immediate material cooperation (with some slight qualification I will mention later on), since this involves joint performance of all or part of the primary act, so it should be ruled out on conscience grounds – at least in situations where the act the cooperator is performing, by its very nature or its unavoidable circumstances, is also wrong. (Where, again, we must remember that what is at issue in conscience cases is cooperation with primary acts that are *held to be wrong* according to the objector's ethical or religious code. This should be taken as implicit throughout the discussion.)

Hence requiring a nurse[1] to hand over surgical instruments for an abortion is impermissible, and is in fact ruled out under the Abortion Act UK's conscience clause. But the same applies to such acts as handing over drugs for the purpose of euthanasia. These are acts of immediate cooperation where they occur as part and parcel of the primary act itself, not as a prior step that lays the conditions for, or facilitates, the primary act to be performed. By their nature (e.g. instruments only used in abortions) or unavoidable circumstances (strong sedatives that have no other use in the situation at hand but to end the patient's life) the acts are wrong, or at least would be considered so by the relevant conscientious objector. Such cooperation, immediate and involving acts to which the cooperator objects in themselves and in the circumstances, deserves the protection of freedom of conscience. Note that the cooperation could be with commissions or omissions; the latter might involve handing over sedatives to keep a patient quiet while they were denied 'artificial nutrition and hydration', otherwise known as food and water. There is no legal protection in the UK from being required by one's medical employer to perform such an act.

When it comes to mediate cooperation, by contrast, we are talking about the supply of *means* or *conditions* for the primary act to take place. The main question is how to balance the loss to be avoided by the cooperator, and the seriousness of the wrong with which they are cooperating,

---

1   We are assuming in all these cases that the cooperator has a conscientious objection to involvement, so I will not state this explicitly.

given the kind of cooperation involved. This delicate balancing act or *proportionality* assessment is how we handle cases such as car pollution: taking your car on a one-minute drive to the corner shop to buy milk generally does not justify the pollution generated. Again, the dentist justifies the moderate pain she causes by the necessity of repairing a damaged tooth. Cooperation cases are not that different.

As a general principle, the more serious the wrong with which you are potentially cooperating, the greater must be the avoidance of loss that cooperation procures. Suppose a nurse considers cosmetic surgery for purely aesthetic reasons a relatively minor wrong with which she would rather not be involved. Were she to be subject to loss of employment for refusing to cooperate, that would clearly outweigh the badness of what she would be involved in, all things being equal. In such a case, it would be morally permissible for her to cooperate, even closely. Suppose, by contrast, she would merely have a day's pay docked for not cooperating: then she would have to 'go with her conscience' and refuse to be involved.

Now consider a pharmacist who refuses to sell the 'morning-after pill' because she knows that sometimes it kills an embryo, a risk of what she considers a very serious wrong. Here, the cost of refusal to cooperate would have to be very high for her to be morally 'off the hook'. Mere loss of pay would be insufficient, but perhaps dismissal from her job would be, at least if it meant an immediate threat to livelihood; for here she would be balancing a *risk* of abortion against the *certainty* of materially serious harm to herself and maybe her family. Now, one might immediately – and quite understandably – tend to become obsessed about these delicate balancing acts. Who's to say whether certainty of unemployment outweighs risk of the death of an embryo? How can anyone know? Isn't this just an exercise in clothing our intuitions or preconceptions with the veneer of theoretical respectability?

The worry is perfectly understandable but equally misplaced. All moral theories, without exception, have to balance various goods and bads, but – if I may be permitted a little sermonising – as Aristotle taught us over two thousand years ago, this is not a mathematical exercise (at least hardly ever, since it's rarely *just* about numbers). We have to look at the situation in front of us, the competing goods and bads, their levels of seriousness or importance, and come to a reasonable judgment. Losses to life and limb are more important than financial losses; serious public harm is worse than serious private harm; certain harms are worse than merely probable or barely possible harms. We need a good deal of 'practical wisdom', as Aristotle and many other philosophers have said, to make decent judgments here, but that does not mean we should avoid them. Moreover, in the grand tradition of the common law we find, in my view, one of the best exemplifications of practical wisdom and good sense applied to complex and factually detailed, real-life cases. A good judge can, as it were, be one of the best judges we have in societies with a common-law tradition.

I want briefly to head off a possible worry the reader might have about this way of looking at cooperation.

Suppose the government, as in the Obamacare mandate, imposes a severe financial penalty on individuals (or groups) for non-cooperation with the performance of some act, say the provision of a service. That penalty, because of its very severity, might in the relevant situation make the individual a permissible cooperator, morally speaking. In which case, doesn't the government have an incentive to impose severe penalties on people for non-cooperation *precisely* in order to ward off conscientious objections? It would be like the fraudster who thinks that if he wants to get a morally upright person to help him embezzle money, it's better to hold a gun to their head than merely threaten moderate violence – not just because it is more likely to work but because the potential cooperator is less likely to refuse due to moral scruples.

This is hardly the outcome that we should want from a general legal and political recognition of the rights of conscience. One solution, I submit, is to be found in the 'strict scrutiny' test of America's Religious Freedom Restoration Act, mentioned earlier. The government needs to have some kind of 'compelling interest' in furthering a given objective that is likely to burden freedom of conscience. It cannot use penalties as a form of *duress* merely to advance whatever objective it sees fit to promote. Secondly, the means used to further that compelling interest need to be the 'least restrictive' available in the circumstances, that is, the least burdensome to freedom of conscience. Put another way, the government should try to minimise the extent to which its promotion of the interest captures conscientious objectors within its net. And if objectors are caught up in the government's advancement of the interest, the burden they are under should not be wholly disproportionate to the value of that interest. In other words, the government should not use its coercive power to play upon the moral scruples of citizens in order to procure their cooperation. The burden the government imposes – say, a financial penalty for failing to assist with furthering a government objective – must reasonably reflect the importance the government attaches to the objective, not merely the eagerness with which it seeks to secure compliance.

Having outlined the general way goods and bads are to be balanced in cooperation cases, we now need to see briefly how factors such as proximity and dispensability apply as part of the overall moral evaluation. The general principle is that the more the cooperator is implicated in the primary act, and the more serious the primary act itself, the more serious the reason they need in order to be morally justified in cooperating. There is no *absolute* judgment to be made here as far as implication goes, only a *comparative* one. What kinds of *hypothetical* cooperation in the circumstances were possible, and how would these compare to the *actual* cooperation being envisaged? So consider a nurse who has scruples about cooperating with some extreme cosmetic surgery that she considers wrong for the patient to undergo. She is worried about whether she should book the patient onto the ward. In one situation, this cooperation could be relatively highly proximate: for suppose she is a senior nurse with total control over who is admitted on a particular day. Suppose this is the only time she will be confronted with this particular patient. If she admits the patient, the patient will certainly be operated on, and if she refuses, then the patient will not, even though he might be operated on at another time when the nurse is away from the ward. Here, her cooperation would be highly proximate inasmuch as her action is causally very close to the operation itself: once the patient is booked in, he is prepped and operated on, with no further bureaucracy or steps needing to be approved. But suppose there were many extra steps: suppose admission had to be followed by all sorts of assessments, approvals, and so on, and the nurse had nothing to do with these. Then her admission of the patient would be relatively remote, causally speaking. You have to compare different possible situations – not just any old situations, but ones that are realistic and reasonably close to the actual circumstances. You also need to compare the nurse's position with that of other actual cooperators: compared to the person who cleans the ward or serves the food, the nurse is a very proximate cooperator; compared to the surgeon who actually performs the operation, she is more remote.

Again, consider dispensability. Suppose the nurse has total control over who is admitted, and that there is no other way for that particular patient to get that particular surgery at that time: the nurse would be an indispensable cooperator. Suppose, on the other hand, that she is one of a number of admitting nurses on a roster, any of whom could admit the patient. If she does not do it, another can and will. Her cooperation would be dispensable, albeit not as dispensable as that of the receptionist who takes the patient's personal details. Suppose there are multiple wards the patient could enter, with the surgeon prepared to perform the operation in any of them. If the nurse refuses to admit, the patient can go to another ward. Her cooperation, again, would be dispensable – far less dispensable than that of the car parking attendant who helps the patient find a parking spot, but more dispensable than the cooperation of the anaesthetist.

We can put forward some general rules for the evaluation of particular cases, once we have determined whether the cooperation is relatively proximate or remote, dispensable or indispensable, whether the primary act is seriously wrong or only a minor wrong, and whether the loss to be avoided by the cooperator is significant or not, given all the circumstances. The overarching rule is: the more serious the wrong with which a person cooperates and the more implicated they are, the greater the reason they need for their cooperation to be justified. You need a more serious reason for cooperating in, say, euthanasia (assuming all the while that the cooperator has a conscientious objection) than in extreme cosmetic surgery. If the cooperation is immediate – a kind of part-performance of the primary act itself – then it *might* be justified if something about the circumstances meant that although the act was wrong for the primary agent to do, it was permissible if done (in part) by the assistant. Imagine a thief who is assisted by a starving man to take food from a supermarket – the starving man having been promised some of the food as an inducement. It is at least arguable that if someone is *genuinely starving*, it is not theft to take food from another, even though it is wrong for the thief to do so. It is, admittedly, not easy to think of cases where immediate material co-operation might be justified, but in principle it may be.

The more indispensable the cooperation, the greater the reason must be for assisting. Again sticking to health care, which is our focus, you need a greater reason for acting as anaesthetist in a sterilisation procedure, assuming no one else can take your place, than for booking in the patient – assuming one of several people could have done that. And the more proximate the cooperation, the greater the reason needed: compare someone who provides information to another on how to commit suicide with someone who sells them the suicide drugs. We should also factor in how *likely* it is that the primary act will occur. You do not need as serious a reason for assisting someone who *might* do something to which you conscientiously object as for assisting someone who definitely will.

When it comes to the reasons for cooperating themselves, we have to look at the goods and bads involved. How serious is the wrong of the primary act? What is the loss to be avoided by cooperating? Inducements involving pressure are all about not suffering some harm – not losing one's job, or one's friends, or even one's life. Material cooperators are trying to avoid harm, and sometimes right-thinking people cannot, and do not have to, resist the pressure unintentionally to assist in bringing about something bad in order to avoid a loss to themselves.

Overall, the seriousness of the reason corresponds to the seriousness of the loss to be avoided. We have to look at the goods and bads and where they reasonably figure in a person's welfare in their particular circumstances.

The loss of a day's wages, say, is moderately serious for the average worker but trivial for a rich person. It might be catastrophic for a poor, third-world farmer. Similarly, the threat of physical pain is usually easier to bear for a soldier than a civilian, and the loss of reputation harder for someone whose livelihood depends on it than for someone whose livelihood does not. A specialist surgeon might find it harder to find alternative employment than a nurse or therapist (though in some situations they might find it easier, due to market demand). We need to take all the facts into consideration and ask whether, in the particular circumstances, the potential loss to the cooperator justified that particular level of cooperation in that particular wrongful act.

Speaking again quite generally, highly proximate, indispensable cooperation in a very serious wrong – perhaps the taking of life or serious bodily harm – could only ever be justified by a very grave risk to the cooperator of a similar magnitude: a gun to the head, as it were. Note that I am not suggesting such cooperation would necessarily be *admirable* or *praiseworthy* – only that it would be *permissible*. In freedom of conscience cases the objector is interested in what they *may* do, not what would bring upon them admiration or praise. The question is whether they should regard their conscience as *troubled*, not their reputation as enhanced. When the primary wrong involves a threat to public safety – assisting a terrorist, for example – it is plausible to claim that one may *never* cooperate since no reason could compare to a potential loss of many lives, but one might also argue that if the cooperation is highly remote and dispensable, say renting a car to the terrorist, a gun at one's head could justify cooperation. Intuitions differ here, so I leave it to the reader to consider.

If the cooperation is dispensable, or not highly proximate, the justification bar is lowered – again, not mathematically, but according to reasonable judgment. There need not be a threat to life and limb, but a more moderate loss like some kind of bodily harm that is more than trivial, or a substantial financial loss that does not amount to serious deprivation. Again, if the cooperation is neither indispensable nor proximate but still involves a serious primary wrong – say, booking in a patient for abortion or sterilisation even though others could have done so and the booking is one of many steps leading to the operation – we should expect that a threat of loss that was perhaps not as serious as the primary wrong but still substantial, such as unemployment or destruction of reputation, might suffice.

When the seriousness of the wrong is decreased, the seriousness of the reason is reduced as well. A conscientious objector needs less reason to cooperate in transgender surgery (assuming they believe it to be harmful and not clinically justified, albeit not life-threatening) than in abortion or euthanasia. Here, a comparable reason might be serious loss of earnings, or disciplinary action by one's employer, say, but the loss need not involve one's entire livelihood, let alone a threat to life and limb. Again, the more proximate and indispensable, the greater the reason needed for assistance. If the cooperation involves relatively minor acts such as cleaning the ward, serving the food, and the like, a minor ticking-off by one's employer is enough to justify involvement.

I hope I have said enough to give the flavour of how co-operation cases should be assessed on the kind of theory I am defending. There is much detail we could go into, looking at various kinds of loss, the different kinds of wrong, and the degree of implication, in order to put more flesh on the bones of the balancing act. There is no room for any of this here: I simply want to persuade the reader that we do have a plausible way of undergirding conscientious objection cases involving cooperation. Most importantly, we do not have to retreat to a purely subjective 'viewpoint' on the matter, as though it were all somehow beyond the bounds of rational thought. Yes, we have to rely to an extent on intuitions and plausible estimations. We have to make fine distinctions in some cases. We have to exercise what the ancient Greek philosophers called 'practical wisdom'. Moreover, we do have people who, on the whole, are pretty darn good at making the sorts of fine distinction, with sensitivity to particular facts but guided by principles, that we need in cooperation cases. They are called *judges*. Why not allow, perhaps over a period of years or decades, a *common law of cooperation* to evolve in response to cases of conscience that come before the courts?

Should you sign? It depends

Signing a document looks like a trivial matter. In one sense it is – no effort required. But it can be momentous. It could be signing someone's death warrant, signing away your life savings, authorising a fraud, deceiving a law enforcement official, approving a dangerous or unethical experiment, and so on. The mere act of signing may or may not make you a cooperator. If committee members sign a policy paper advising the government to do such and such, they will not be actual *assistants* in the government's execution of the policy. Signing, in order to amount to cooperation, needs to supply means or conditions for the primary act to be performed. If Mike's signature is required for the imprisonment of an innocent man unfairly convicted, his cooperation will be dispensable if any of a number of people could have signed and Mike just happened to be the first available person. If he is the prison governor and only his signature will do, his cooperation is indispensable and he is more closely implicated as a result. If no more hurdles have to be cleared between signing and incarceration, the governor's cooperation is highly proximate.

Now consider a conscientious objector in wartime. Usually, conscientious objectors have to register as such at or around the time their country enters into military conflict. They need to give the government their name, perhaps being required to enlist in some non-combat role as a substitute. Registering in this way does not make the objector a *cooperator* in the war, even though the causal result of their opting out is that another soldier is drafted in their place (assuming conscription). The conscientious objector is precisely *opting out* of military service rather than *assisting* the government to find a replacement, let alone assisting it to fight a war. If explicitly opting out of some activity ipso facto made a person a cooperator in that activity, then the very idea of opting out would lose all meaning: it would create a Hotel California situation, where you could enter but never leave. At least, you could never leave without having by definition to be morally scrupulous about what you were doing. The concentration camp prisoner who opted out of working in the crematorium in favour of working in the camp hospital (assuming such choices were ever available) would have had to wonder whether the very act of opting out, which would have resulted in the co-option of a replacement worker in the crematorium, was a form of assistance to those running the camp. More generally, it would mean that on very many occasions where you refused to assist in some action, there was a live moral question about whether by refusing you were *still* assisting. This is highly implausible.

Now consider a variation on the above wartime scenario. In 1863, the US federal government's Civil War Enrolment Act permitted a draftee to avoid service by either providing a substitute or paying $300. Here, providing a substitute to serve in the conscientious objector's place *would* have been a case of cooperation, since the objector would have been himself providing *means* by which the war could be prosecuted. He would not have been doing this intentionally, of course, so he would only have been a material cooperator. The objector's cooperation would have been highly proximate, since soldiers and weapons are the most proximate *means* of fighting a war (they certainly were in 1863!); so their supply would have been causally about as close as can be to prosecution of the war itself. It would, however, have been *dispensable* on the assumption that the state had many ways of finding and drafting combatants without having to rely on a conscientious objector's opt-out.

As for the losses, in this case the objector had to provide a substitute or else pay what was then a hefty fine (equivalent to over $5,000 now and to over 100 days' average wages then). In general, the loss of a substantial portion of one's livelihood over a protracted period of time gives a serious prima facie reason for cooperation. This can be defeated, however, by the seriousness of the wrong in which the cooperator is potentially implicated and their overall role in it. The conscientious objector generally regards war as a whole, or some particular war, as a very serious evil. (Whether they are correct is irrelevant since we are, remember, *not judging* the cooperator's moral views about the primary act.) The loss of a substantial portion of one's income could plausibly be a serious enough reason for many kinds of cooperation; but wartime conscientious objectors consider themselves to be potential cooperators in wrongful killing, which outweighs a mere financial penalty. On the other hand, the role played by the objector in this case, though proximate, would be highly dispensable and also a *very small part* of the overall enterprise – the supply of a single replacement soldier. As such, it is quite reasonable to think that cooperation would be morally permissible in this sort of case.

Now, I may be wrong about this. There might be other plausible ways of assessing all the factors, and the particular facts of the case are, as always, crucial. As I said earlier, 'doing morality', as it were, is not doing maths. There is no ethical calculator that will spew out a correct result, much as some philosophers these days would like it to be so. Still, the general outlines are clear enough, and there is much more that can be said. If the courts were to give this sort of reasoning about cooperation the attention it deserved, a rich jurisprudence on the subject would surely develop over time.

5 APPLICATION TO CONTESTED CASES

Hobby Lobby: what it got right, what it got wrong

In 2017, Judge Neil Gorsuch of the US Court of Appeals was confirmed as a member of the US Supreme Court. He was questioned during his confirmation hearings about his judgment in *Hobby Lobby v. Sebelius*, federal court precursor to the Supreme Court *Hobby Lobby* case mentioned earlier. Recall that in *Hobby Lobby* the question was whether a small, family-owned corporation was being substantially burdened in its religious freedom under the Religious Freedom Restoration Act. President Obama's healthcare law required employers to provide health insurance that also covered contraception, including abortifacient methods. The corporation's owners sincerely believed the use of such methods violated their deeply held religious beliefs, and the Supreme Court concurred.

In his confirmation hearing, Judge Gorsuch reiterated his agreement with the decision. Somewhat self-effacingly, he said: 'If we got it wrong, I'm sorry.' He was, of course, referring to the fact that some people might think the *Hobby Lobby* owners should not have received an 'accommodation' allowing them to opt out of the contraceptive mandate. In my view, he – and the Supreme Court – got something wrong, but not that. More precisely, they came to the right decision but for the wrong reasons. On the assumption that what the owners objected to was morally wrong – abortifacient contraception – they would have been illicit cooperators by purchasing the insurance.

It might plausibly be thought that purchasing health insurance to cover employees engaged in wrongful activity would not itself be a morally indifferent act. This would rule out the cooperation from the start as being *implicitly formal*: by purchasing insurance that contains cover for wrongful activity as an *essential element*, the owners would have been, by their conduct, tacitly approving of their employees' wrongful behaviour without explicitly doing so. It would be like the case of a juror who does not explicitly intend to condemn an innocent man, but goes ahead and votes guilty due to pressure from his fellow jurors.

Suppose, on the other hand, that purchase of the insurance was itself morally neutral. Still, the employers would be material but proximate cooperators in serious wrongdoing, without a reason sufficient to outweigh the gravity of what they were potentially involved in. Purchasing insurance to cover an activity is generally proximate assistance since it facilitates, financially, the performance of the activity. Short of actual physical or medical assistance, when it comes to health-related activity, financial help is probably the next closest kind of assistance. The financial penalties for non-compliance were severe, however, perhaps threatening the survival of the corporation itself and the livelihoods of many people. Yet it is hard to see how proximate cooperation in the taking of life – the destruction of embryos – can be justified by a pecuniary penalty for refusing.

So, on an objective theory of cooperation such as I am defending, the owners do come out as illicit cooperators. Given that they met the test of the RFRA for a substantial burden on their religious exercise (such cooperation being imposed in a way that was not the least restrictive means for the government to pursue its 'compelling interest' in contraceptive cover), the decision reached by the court was correct. The problem, however, is that it did *not* employ such a theory. Rather, it treated the owners' belief that they would be illicit cooperators as *itself a religious belief* whose mere *sincerity* was sufficient to bring it within the religious freedom protection afforded by federal statute.

In fact, Judge Gorsuch put it best himself in the lower-court judgment: 'As they [the company owners] understand it, ordering their companies to provide insurance coverage for drugs or devices whose use is inconsistent with their faith *itself* violates their faith, representing a degree of complicity their religion disallows' (Hobby Lobby 2013: 79). In other words, he treated – as did the Supreme Court – the very question of whether the plaintiffs were illicit cooperators as *itself* purely a matter of religious faith.

Why is this important? The problem derives from the fact that American courts, as with most Western courts, do not as a matter of legal principle *question* the religious beliefs of a litigant seeking to protect their religious freedom (see, for example, Thomas 1981; Hernandez 1989).

That is, they do not look behind the *sincerity* of the belief to question its *reasonableness*. This means that if a plaintiff complains that a certain law or regulation makes them a cooperator in wrongdoing, the court does not question whether this belief is reasonable or not. The only question, for American courts, is whether the law or regulation violates RFRA by imposing a 'substantial burden' on religious freedom.

Given what I have been arguing, however, there is a plausible way of theorising about cooperation that does not make it a religious matter as such. True, the ethics of cooperation I have been defending, and of which the Supreme Court took notice in *Hobby Lobby*, was developed by Catholic theologians who thought long and hard about 'cases of conscience'. Their theory is found in textbooks of moral theology and is often, unsurprisingly, applied to matters of religious doctrine. But it is also applied to cases that we would recognise as purely secular, such as whether it is permissible to sell a weapon to an intoxicated man, or help a burglar steal valuable documents. (See McHugh and Callan (1958: 615–41) for the theory and many examples both religious and secular.)

When broaching the issue, the Supreme Court said: 'This belief [that providing insurance cover for contraception under the mandate] implicates a difficult and important question of religion and moral philosophy, namely, the circumstances under which it is wrong for a person to perform an act that is innocent in itself but that has the effect of enabling or facilitating the commission of an immoral act by another.' The Court added a footnote citing my own previous work along with some theology textbooks (Burwell 2014: 36 and note 34). But instead of using these works as guidance in reaching a decision as to whether such a belief was reasonable, the Court took them as evidence that the very question of cooperation was primarily religious in nature – or if philosophical, then tied essentially to religion. They declined to analyse the question but instead placed the plaintiffs' belief within the category of 'sincerely held religious belief', and as such not to be second-guessed. Hence being required by the government to violate that belief was ipso facto a requirement to violate their religion. In my view, this is a recipe for significant future problems that will undermine religious freedom itself.

Zubik v. Burwell: an opt-out or a trigger?

How could that be? Let us go back to *Zubik v. Burwell*, which was the consolidation of a number of lower-court cases including most famously *Little Sisters of the Poor v. Burwell*, in which a religious non-profit organisation also objected to the contraceptive mandate as substantially burdensome to freedom of religion under RFRA (Little Sisters 2015). The difference from *Hobby Lobby*, however, is crucial: in *Hobby Lobby* the Supreme Court held that the objectors (owners of closely held, for-profit corporations) were entitled to what they requested, namely the same accommodation granted to religious non-profits, allowing them to opt out of providing the relevant insurance coverage. The objectors in *Little Sisters of the Poor* and then in *Zubik*, however, objected to *the very accommodation itself.*

The accommodation provided by the government required a conscientious objector to notify either the government or the objector's insurance company (we can leave aside the complexities) that they opted out of the mandate and would not provide contraceptive coverage. It was then up to the government or the insurance company to step in and fill the gap. But the objectors in *Little Sisters* and related cases, and then in *Zubik*, considered the very act of *opting out* to be illicit cooperation, relying precisely on *Hobby Lobby* for their argument.

Why would they think that? The objectors wanted no part whatsoever in any activity that 'triggered' contraceptive coverage, as they put it (Little Sisters 2015: 55). They saw the opt-out as 'involving' them, or making them 'complicit', in the objectionable activity. They sincerely held this belief, considering it part of their religious exercise, and so claimed that the opt-out substantially burdened that exercise. They did not have to name an alternative insurer or put any means in place for the coverage to be provided; all they needed to do was provide their own name and state that they opted out of providing the coverage themselves. Yet they objected to this very act.

The appellate court, however, rejected the plaintiffs' argument. The opt-out was not a 'trigger' or cause of the objectionable coverage. It was in no way a means of implementing the coverage but solely a way for the plaintiffs to *extricate* themselves from involvement. How else was the government supposed to know what to do if they did not at least know who was opting out? The government could perhaps have taken it upon themselves to notify employees of their right to contraceptive coverage under a government plan, supplemental to the employer policy, and without the employer having to do anything but provide their own acceptable coverage. But that was not the scheme the government put in place. There is little doubt that the plaintiffs objected to that very scheme, and would have preferred an alternative that did not even require them to opt out. This is understandable, and no doubt worth campaigning for by conscientious objectors, but it did not justify the argument that, given the scheme in place, an opt-out was a form of illicit cooperation.

Why is this mistaken argument by the plaintiffs a problem? Because it treats their belief about whether they are cooperating illicitly as *itself* a matter of religion, when it is not. Since religious beliefs are not subjected to a reasonableness test by the courts, the mere fact that a plaintiff *sincerely* holds a particular religious belief is enough for that belief to be within the scope of RFRA and the First Amendment. Judge Baldock, who dissented in part from the majority in *Little Sisters* (for complex reasons that need not detain us), put his finger on the problem without recognising it *as* a problem. Quoting Judge Kavanaugh in a similar case, Baldock said: 'But what if the religious organizations are misguided in thinking that this scheme … makes them complicit in facilitating contraception or abortion? That is not our call to make under the first prong of RFRA' (Priests for Life 2015: 8). Baldock added: 'And *Hobby Lobby* supports this position well, as questioning a religious adherent's understanding of the significance of a compelled action comes dangerously close to questioning "whether the religious belief asserted in a RFRA case is reasonable" – a "question that the federal courts have no business addressing"' (Little Sisters 2015: 111).

Strictly, then, if a conscientious objector *sincerely believes* he is cooperating impermissibly, and if that belief is not subject to any test of reasonableness, it must be protected under law – no matter how unreasonable it is. All things being equal, to believe that opting out is just such a case of cooperation is unreasonable – as unreasonable as thinking that by running away from a riot you are cooperating with the rioters. Now, running away *might* in the circumstances be an act of cowardice, or in some other way undesirable. Similarly, one might protest against having to opt out of the contraceptive mandate because one objected to the entire Obamacare scheme, with its use of private insurers to carry out the government's 'dirty work', as it were. But the way to combat that is not by preventing an objective assessment of whether one is cooperating illicitly. It is by the usual means for trying to overturn objectionable laws – the ballot box, parliamentary process, protest; perhaps even civil disobedience.

By acknowledging the existence of a theory of cooperation, as the Supreme Court did in *Hobby Lobby*, but refusing to use it in fear of 'second-guessing' the plaintiffs' religious beliefs, the court effectively set the stage for a possible judicial *backlash* against the very conscientious objectors they were trying to accommodate. In fact, the *Little Sisters* case, along with related cases, made it to the Supreme Court – only for the court to *vacate* all previous judgments, including the fair and reasonable one discussed above, and send the whole issue back to the parties and lower courts for yet further negotiation and resolution. This is where matters stand at the time of writing, and my fear is that the courts, worried that the 'mere sincerity' test of *Hobby Lobby* will open the floodgates to even the most far-fetched conscience cases, will find ways around that test and thereby undermine the very freedoms the test was supposed to protect. Adopting a plausible, relatively well worked-out theory of cooperation along the lines I have defended could prevent just such a backlash.

Doogan and Wood cannot stand

As we saw, the UK Supreme Court in *Doogan and Wood* limited freedom of religion and conscience in abortion cases to actual *participation* in the abortion process, as laid down by the Abortion Act 1967. The Glasgow midwives believed that 'any involvement in the process of termination render[ed] them accomplices to and culpable for that grave offence' (Doogan 2014: 7). In particular, they objected to 'delegating, supervising and/or supporting staff to participate in and provide care to patients throughout the termination process', arguing that these were forms of 'participation'.

Unsurprisingly, the court disagreed. The 'treatment' under the Act, which gave rise to a conscience exemption for participation, could only refer to the abortion process itself, a 'whole course of medical treatment' beginning, if required, with the administration of labour-inducing drugs and ending with 'delivery of the foetus, placenta and membrane' (Doogan 2014: 14). Participation was interpreted as meaning part-performance, and the object of the part-performance was the specific activity that had been illegal before the Act and was made lawful by it – namely, the act of termination itself, at any stage from beginning to end but not including ancillary supervisory, pastoral, administrative or managerial activities.

Given the law as it stands, it is hard to see how the court could have arrived at any other result. To have extended conscience protection to ancillary activities that were clearly not 'participation in treatment' would have been to stretch the meaning of words, and the intent of Parliament, beyond what was reasonable. This does not, however, make the result satisfactory from the viewpoint of freedom of religion and conscience. Supervising an abortion ward, making bookings, managing shifts, offering psychological support before and after the abortion, are all forms of *co-operation* even if they are not actual participation in the treatment itself. As such, they should come under the umbrella of freedom of conscience if freedom of conscience is to have any substantial meaning at all.

Similarly to the US, however, in the UK there is no jurisprudence of cooperation – nothing that the courts *could* have drawn on to allay the concerns of Lady Hale herself, the author of the judgment in *Doogan*, that a 'reasonable accommodation' has yet to be found between freedom of religion and conscience, on the one hand, and competing rights on the other. This is where judicial notice of the principles of cooperation would have helped. Note first that abortion is but one among many activities within health care where conscientious objections will undoubtedly arise. What about euthanasia? Transgender surgery? Extreme cosmetic surgery? Apotemnophilia (the persistent desire for the amputation of a healthy limb)? What about the whole issue of a conscientious objector's *referring* a patient to another, willing practitioner? Surely the approach of 'one conscience clause at a time' would be a highly undesirable way to proceed. In which case, doesn't the law need a more general way of dealing with conscience cases, preferably with statutory backing?

Consider what the court might have been able to say in *Doogan* had the judges been able to rely on a general theory of cooperation. They might have been in a position to hold, for example, that arranging the night shift or managing rest breaks on the ward was remote, dispensable, material cooperation for which a serious reason, such as loss of employment, existed. It would be, so the thought goes, remote because managing shifts and breaks would go on with or without abortions taking place, and such activity has no 'executive character' about it: it does not involve supplying tools or means by which the specific act of abortion takes place. It might be thought dispensable because although the ward could not operate in any respect without a system of shifts and breaks, it might be that no particular midwife needed to manage it since the skills required were fairly generic. (Dispensability concerns both what is done and by whom.) On the other hand, the court might also have held that booking a specific patient in for an abortion was proximate cooperation since this would involve setting the particular process in motion leading to the objectionable primary act. In this respect, booking in a patient provides a tool by which an abortion can take place. It might also be thought indispensable inasmuch as a booking system is a practical causal necessity for any specific procedure to take place, unlike shift management that applies across the board, even if any midwife could operate the booking system. Whatever the court might have said about the indispensability of booking, actual admission of the patient onto the ward would seem to be indispensable cooperation, part of the very means by which the abortion must eventually take place. Proximate, indispensable material cooperation would require a very serious reason to be permitted. Given that what the midwives objected to was the ending of a life, it is hard to see how anything short of a threat to their own lives would have justified cooperating (for further discussion, see Oderberg 2017a).

I am less concerned here with the specific case at hand than with drawing a lesson about what might be achieved by a judicially noticed and developed ethics of cooperation. The courts, especially if they had a statutory framework on which to fall back, could avoid piecemeal recognition of freedom of religion and conscience confined to individual conscience clauses, as compared with the universal right to abortion, say, or transgender surgery, currently recognised by the law. This would put freedom of religion and conscience on a relatively equal footing with these other legal rights, at least as far as cooperation is concerned—which is where the litigation is increasingly directed.

Equality Acts and regulations: a charter for inequality

In the UK, as in many other countries, there has been a myriad of equality statutes and regulations designed to require 'equal treatment' for various categories of persons who, for whatever reason, have not previously received it or need to have it reinforced by law. The Equality Act 2010 codifies most of the pre-existing equality and anti-discrimination law and regulations in the UK. It provides a list of 'protected characteristics', whereby any person (or group) who discriminates directly or indirectly against a person (or group) with a protected characteristic acts unlawfully. The protected characteristics are: age; disability; gender reassignment; marriage and civil partnership; pregnancy and maternity; race; religion or belief; sex; and sexual orientation.

One would think that, on the face of it, and by its very intent, people with protected characteristics would be treated equally to each other as well as to those without protected characteristics. This does not, however, seem to be the reality. Consider again *Bull v. Hall*, the case of the Christian guest house owners who refused a room to a same-sex couple in a civil partnership. The UK Supreme Court, with Lady Hale writing the main judgment, dismissed the Christian guest house owners' appeal against the earlier finding of discrimination. Although the facts of the case arose before the Equality Act, the prior sexual orientation and related regulations in force at the time were largely the same.

There is no room to analyse the case in detail, but we should still notice the unequal treatment in the decision. Some of the judges found direct discrimination, which is always unlawful. Others found indirect discrimination, whereby although the Christian owners did not *single out* the gay couple for unequal treatment on grounds of sexual orientation, the *effect* of their refusal to rent a room was to disadvantage homosexual couples as a class. Indirect discrimination could be justified as a 'proportionate means of achieving a legitimate aim' (Bull 2013: 13), but no such justification was recognised. Be that as it may, the result was that the Christian owners were not allowed to choose who they could and could not admit into their establishment on the basis of their religious beliefs. Article 9 of the European Convention states that '[f]reedom to manifest one's religion or beliefs shall be subject only to such limitations as are prescribed by law and are necessary in a democratic society for the ... protection of the rights and freedoms of others.' Fundamentally, the court saw the implementation of the equality law against the Christian owners as just such a necessary limitation protecting the rights of the gay couple.

But what rights of the gay couple are at issue? It cannot be the right not to be discriminated against by others, including Christians, since that would make the argument circular: the guest house owners were guilty of discrimination on the grounds that they violated the right of the gay couple not to be discriminated against. Rather, what was at issue was 'equal treatment', that is, the equal right to goods and services freely available to those without protected characteristics. The problem, though, is that – as the court noted in passing – the gay couple found alternative accommodation. So they were not denied access to accommodation as such, only to accommodation in a *particular* guest house. Surely, though, that also constitutes unequal treatment? Consider, however, that the guest house owners were penalised for not being allowed to manifest a *particular* religious belief, namely their belief concerning sexual morality and the necessity of not acting against it in practice. That particular belief was not given equal treatment. Still, one may object, what was at issue was the availability of goods and services: the owners were restricting availability for the homosexual couple, but penalising the owners did not prevent them from running their business, that is, providing whatever goods and services they wanted. Yet there clearly *was* a restriction here. The owners were not themselves seeking goods or services, to be sure, but they were seeking to *control their own* goods and services. They were being compelled to provide – or penalised for not providing – their goods and services to a particular customer. So just as the owners were seeking to restrict availability, the couple were seeking to control provision; yet it is hard to see why availability is more important, legally or morally, than provision – or vice versa. I will come back to this issue later, since it raises some profoundly important questions.

A similar case involves the so-called 'Christian bakers' in Northern Ireland (the *Ashers Baking Company* case) who refused to sell to a gay man a cake with a message on it supporting homosexual marriage (Ashers 2016). The

Court of Appeal found for the gay man, holding that the bakers had directly discriminated against him on grounds of sexual orientation under the Northern Ireland equality regulations. Once again I have no space to delve into the details of this rather curiously reasoned judgment, so I will note only the same general concern. It is hard to see how equality was achieved in this case given that the bakers themselves had the Article 9 right, as the court put it, 'to hold and manifest their genuinely held religious belief that marriage is, according to God's law, between one man and one woman'.

The court saw no need to 'read down' the equality regulations to protect freedom of religion. Rather, what they did was to read down the *bakers'* right to 'manifest [their] religion or belief ... in practice' (ECHR terminology). Why the partiality for one right over another? It might be replied: because otherwise the gay man would have been denied goods and services legally available to everyone else. Again, however, just as the couple in the guest house case had no trouble finding alternative accommodation, so the man in the bakery case had no trouble finding another baker happy to sell him a cake with the pro-gay marriage message he wanted. Still, the man in the bakery case was being denied *particular* goods and services from a *particular* provider. True, but the court denied the bakers the right to manifest their religious belief in respect of *particular* customers on a *particular* occasion.

I am going to look at this sort of question in more detail in the following two chapters, since I now want to broaden the discussion significantly. We have looked at conscientious objection and freedom of religion with special focus on the health-care context. I have argued that the courts, and preferably legislatures as well, should adopt a theory of cooperation of the sort I have outlined, so as to contribute to forging a *reasonable* balance between proper protection for freedom of conscience and religion on the one hand and duties laid down by law on the other. Objectors would be given a protection they currently do not have – from being *illicit cooperators* in activities to which they object. But this would not rule out all forms of cooperation, as long as the cooperation was sufficiently remote, dispensable, mediate, and so on, and the loss to be avoided by the cooperator was proportionate to the gravity of the primary activity to which they objected.

Clearly, however, the fairly specific issues discussed so far threaten to stir up a hornet's nest of broader and even more controversial questions concerning the balancing of freedoms in diverse, pluralistic, liberal societies. How 'involved' should a person or group be *required* to be in the activities or expression of values of another person or group? How does such a question relate to the more fundamental matter of freedom of association? In the next chapter I will broach these broader questions, and in the final chapter I will return to something more tangible – policy proposals that give freedom of conscience and religion more solid protection than they currently have.

6 FREEDOM OF CONSCIENCE: HOW FAR CAN IT GO?

Pluralism to the rescue?

Most Western societies, and certainly the UK and US, are liberal, secular and pluralistic. This means that there are many different groupings within society, whether by religion, race, cultural background, origin, political or moral beliefs, lifestyle, and so on. Liberal society is dedicated to preserving, in a peaceful and harmonious way, the balance between competing interests possessed by these groups. Equality and anti-discrimination laws are part of the way liberalism seeks to achieve this.

It is not, however, only about harmonising or balancing competing interests. Many of the rights and freedoms protected by equality and anti-discrimination laws are already given fundamental legal protection in the international treaties and conventions to which the UK, US and most other Western societies have signed up. Freedom of religion and of political belief are two freedoms already considered basic in international law. Domestic equality laws simply enshrine what was already recognised by Western societies as requiring protection.

Trade-offs are unavoidable, of course. Some are perfectly acceptable by liberal standards. For example, suppose Muslims want to build a mosque in location A, but Baptists also want to build a church in the same place. Suppose there is a large Muslim population in A but few Baptists. Or suppose there are few Muslims and many Baptists, but the Baptists already have several churches in the vicinity of A, so that no Baptist need go without a church to attend. A planning committee would act reasonably by awarding permission to the Muslims but not the Baptists. Would the committee be discriminating against the Baptists? It is hard to see how, given that it was meeting the greater need rather than making a judgment about which religion is better or more deserving in itself. Moreover, on the second scenario the Baptists would have what I shall call 'full and fair access' to the facilities they needed, so disallowing an additional church at location A would disadvantage them hardly at all.

It is not these sorts of trade-off that we should consider problematic. There is a spectrum of trade-offs when it comes to balancing competing interests, but the ones I have in mind strike deeply at the very rights liberal societies should be seeking to protect. When it comes to freedom of religion and conscience, what we now see are laws and court decisions that (a) impinge upon matters of fundamental principle and (b) constitute an ongoing, systematic pattern of reducing those freedoms to things with little substance or meaning. In the US, we saw that the Obamacare 'contraceptive mandate' was a requirement by the federal government that employers with non-negotiable, principled objections based on religion and morality provide, on pain of severe penalty, certain kinds of employee health insurance. In the UK, we saw that the midwives in *Doogan* had no leeway when it came to avoiding involvement in practices they deemed completely wrong according to their sincere and deeply held beliefs.

There can be no doubt that the secularist trend in modern liberalism underlies, in large part, the fact that religious believers are increasingly on the back foot when it comes to securing protection for their beliefs. More and more prominently do we find, for instance, medical or semi-medical professional bodies asserting that the religious or ethical scruples of individual practitioners should not stand in the way of providing services to patients, who have an inviolable right to whatever is legally available and is deemed – by the government, perhaps, or by the 'medical consensus', or by the professional body itself – to be 'in the best interests' of patients. For a recent example, at the time of writing the General Pharmaceutical Council (GPhC) is holding a consultation on whether pharmacists should be allowed, by their code of practice, to refuse any service based on their 'religion, personal values or beliefs' (GPhC 2016). The Council's recommendation is that pharmacists should not be so allowed.

Now, we can understand how it would hardly be reasonable for a pharmacist to say, 'I want to be a pharmacist but I will not as a matter of conscience dispense medicines', or for a doctor to insist on practising medicine while refusing on 'religious grounds' to check anyone's pulse! Sometimes it is just part of one's job to do certain things, and if one's conscience – however bizarrely – forbids perfectly reasonable activities that are essential to the job, then the freedom not to take the job suffices for freedom of conscience. No one has a *right*, whether in law or morality, to any particular job.

We also recognise, however, that there are serious moral issues, many of them with decades of heated debate behind them, with regard to which refusal to be involved (including by illicit cooperation) looks perfectly reasonable and something liberal society should accommodate. Furthermore, there are *new* debates, and ones that have not even commenced yet but are on the horizon, concerning activities, procedures and technologies, where an accommodation for conscience is the only sane thing a liberal state could provide. Nor would one need to be a religious believer at all to regard such an accommodation as both reasonable and necessary. I mentioned earlier extreme cosmetic surgery, transgender surgery, healthy limb amputation, and so on. We will see further debates about 'neuro-enhancers', e.g. drugs that give people a 'cognitive advantage' over others, and other forms of bio-enhancement and life-extension technology. The list is probably endless. Yet society is nowhere close to providing the sorts of accommodation needed to give practical meaning to the many principled religious or ethical objections that people will have to being involved with such things.

What, then, is the meaning of pluralism? Surely it cannot be: 'You can have your religion or your morality; just remember that the secular liberal state ultimately determines whether it is to be respected.' Nor can it be:

'All groups in our pluralistic society are equal; it's just that some are more equal than others.' A liberal state, on any reasonable conception, is not a secular authoritarian state. A secular authoritarian state will relegate religion to a position of ineffectuality, where believers' rights are always trumped by the secular values deemed correct by that state, unless they harmonise completely with those values. A liberal state – one where no value system is the *official* value system of the state – will give full respect to freedom of religion and belief along with the other freedoms, such as of speech, of the press, and of election, that traditionally characterise liberalism in all its forms. A plurality of interest groups in a liberal state means a plurality of value systems and, hence, a plurality of freedoms for each system.

There is, however, nothing in what I have said that implies that freedom of religion means the freedom to do just *anything* that a person sincerely believes to be part of their religious code. Freedom of speech is a basic right, but only an absolutist libertarian would say that a person has the right to say whatever they want, whenever they want, such as advocacy of crime, of the assassination of politicians, and so on. Nor do many people think the media have the right to report whatever they want, such as sensitive state secrets, or the private contact details of innocent people. To make an exception for religion and conscience would be to privilege this freedom over the others, and I am not advocating this.

Now, where the line is drawn is of course a difficult and sensitive matter, and reaching a consensus in a pluralistic society will always be tricky. Nor do I pretend to offer a simple solution here. There are, however, some guiding principles that should be followed if freedom of religion and conscience are to be taken seriously – more seriously than they are at present. One is that there should be a presumption in favour of the freedom in this specific sense: the legal protection should embody the idea that conscientious objection is presumed to be sincere unless proven otherwise. Another presumption should be that what is objected to genuinely belongs to a religious or ethical code unless proven otherwise. (Being a mere customary practice is not, in my view, enough.) A further presumption should be that what is objected to is something over which there is a history of dispute between recognised bodies of thought or over which reasonable people have disagreed or could disagree.

As well as these presumptions, and perhaps more important, are the following two principles. First, freedom of religion and conscience, at least where health care is concerned, primarily governs refraining from the performance of, and cooperation with, acts prescribed or permitted by the relevant laws or professional guidelines. It governs, to a far lesser extent, the doing of certain things. The reason should be clear. When a conscientious objector asks to refrain from involvement in some practice, that does not – as I will emphasise shortly – prevent the other person, such as the patient, from being subject to that practice at the hands of someone else – one who does not object to it. If an objector can opt out, then someone else can opt in. If the patient wants that act to be performed, there will always be someone else to do it. This is especially true in a pluralistic society and is rightly seen by liberals as one of its advantages. By contrast, when a person seeks the protection of freedom of religion and conscience to *do* something to someone else, that other person is trapped, legally speaking. Consider the horrific practice of female genital mutilation. If a Muslim or other[1] doctor were to have the protection of freedom of religion to perform it, how could the victim have legal protection against it?[2] Where could they turn? So we should require that the use of freedom of religion and conscience to *do* something to someone else carries a higher burden of proof from the person petitioning for it that the act is not objectively harmful.[3]

Secondly, freedom of conscience and religion applies only if the protection afforded the objector does not entail that they behave in a way that is clearly *inconsistent with exercise of their profession*. For instance, freedom of religion and conscience do not entail that a conscientious objector should be protected in their sincere belief that curing patients or doing anything to improve their physical welfare is wrong. That would hardly be consistent with acting as a health-care professional in the first place. Of course, there are more subtle and sensitive cases. Many would argue that conscience protection

---

1   Note that FGM is not exclusively a Muslim practice, but most FGM occurs in predominantly Muslim countries and communities.

2   Assuming that a parent or guardian was objecting on the child's behalf.

3   The objector might additionally be required to show *beyond reasonable doubt*, rather than on a balance of probabilities, that FGM was part of a historic religious or ethical code as opposed to a mere customary practice.

against providing, say, abortion services is inconsistent with the requirements of health care; that freedom not to provide such a service, when requested legally, is inconsistent with a doctor's or nurse's role as a health-care professional. Many would argue the exact opposite: that abortion harms the person who undergoes it, no matter what that person may *think* about their situation (leaving aside the belief by all objectors to abortion that it involves taking a human life). Yet others would take a neutral or agnostic stance on the matter. The existence of such long-standing and robust disagreement, even if one or other side is in the numerical minority, demonstrates that there is no *clear* inconsistency with professional duty in being granted conscience protection in such a situation. In many conscience cases, especially those that come before the courts, one or other party will appeal to the 'demands' of the profession to justify their position. This is in the nature of such cases. In general, though, it is a fairly high bar to cross in order to show that a particular activity that is the subject of genuine conscientious objection *must* be performed if a health-care worker is to act in accordance with their professional requirements. Needless to say, those requirements are not simply what happens to be written down in professional guidelines. This is important evidence of the view of the profession at a moment in time. But the profession would need first to absorb the requirements of a legal framework for conscientious protection, such as I am advocating, *before* coming to a settled view about what duties, exactly, the profession of health-care worker absolutely requires.

Freedom of dissociation

I now want to focus on perhaps the most important freedom of all in a liberal society – freedom of association. Freedom of association is another one of the rights always officially recognised in liberal societies. The UN's Universal Declaration on Human Rights puts it as follows[4]: '(1) Everyone has the right to freedom of peaceful assembly and association; (2) No one may be compelled to belong to an association'. The European Convention on Human Rights says[5]: 'Everyone has the right to freedom of peaceful assembly and to freedom of association with others...', followed by a specific reference to trades unions and the listing of many exceptions based on law, public safety, national security, and so on – to the point of making the right seem not very contentful. That aside for now, the wording of such statements seems narrow – confined explicitly or implicitly to trades unions, political organisations, and other semi-public bodies. But the right surely is not that narrow, whatever we think of the way it is worded in conventions and declarations.

The right to free association includes such things as (and some of these are also recognised in international documents): the right to choose your friends, the right to choose your spouse and start a family, the right to choose where you live, with whom you socialise, who you let onto

---

4   Article 20: http://www.un.org/en/universal-declaration-human-rights/ [last accessed 26.10.17].

5   Article 11, sec. 1: http://www.echr.coe.int/Documents/Convention_ENG. pdf [last accessed 26.10.17].

your property, where you shop, where you enjoy leisure time, your business relationships, political associations, and more. Clearly, freedom of association is a broad right, whatever limitations it may be subject to. Note that freedom to choose where and with whom you do business is reflected in the legal right to freedom of contract, but this specific right is founded on the moral right to freedom of association. The same for the freedom to choose whom to let on your land, where the right to property presupposes freedom of association. Without freedom of association, or – more realistically – with severe curtailment of the right, totalitarianism is a likely consequence. One of the hallmarks of a totalitarian regime is its coercion of membership in officially approved organisations only and dissolution of the rest. Another is its virtually total surveillance, which severely constricts a person's choice of friends, associates, and even family. Totalitarianism contains the denial of freedom of association at its core. So I think we can all agree that freedom of association is a fundamental right, albeit not without limits – as with all basic rights.

The limits of freedom of association are not, however, my focus. Rather, I am interested here in the converse of freedom of association – what I call freedom of *dissociation*. After all, if we are free to associate with whomever we choose, why are we not free to dissociate from whomever we choose? Just as I am free to choose my friends, so I am free to drop them; just as I am free to join a trade union, a political party, or a gym, so I am free to end my membership. Nor am I required to join in the first place. So by dissociation I mean both non-association and withdrawal from association. People are free to marry or remain single, and they are also free under law to separate or divorce. Some religions forbid divorce, and one may debate the ethics of divorce, but that's not the point; we have already noted that issues arise over where limitations are to be drawn. My point is simply that there is a moral right to freedom of dissociation, and that the law reflects this.

How does freedom of dissociation tie in to freedom of religion and conscience? I suggest that freedom of religion and conscience in a liberal society can be looked at as a manifestation or aspect of the fundamental freedom of dissociation (and also, of course, of its correlate – freedom of association). This, at least, is how a liberal society ought to look at freedom of religion and conscience, *politically* speaking. Religious believers themselves have more basic reasons for maintaining their freedom of conscience with regard to certain activities, ones specific to their religious values (each believes their religion to be true, to contain various commandments, and so on). But from a political point of view, in a liberal, pluralistic society, both believers and non-believers should see freedom of conscience as an aspect of freedom of dissociation – whatever religiously specific values undergird this freedom for believers themselves.

A person, whether within the health-care field or outside it, who objects in conscience to being involved or implicated in a certain activity, or practice, or service, is in effect saying that they don't want to be associated with it or the people who are trying to involve the objector in it. By 'associated' I do not mean something as loose as being in the same room or building, or sharing the same sandwich counter, or some such. I mean something more specific: namely, being associated in a way that is troubling to their conscience on grounds of principle, whereby the objector would be involved in actual wrongdoing if they maintained such involvement.

Now, as I have been arguing in respect of health care, some forms of cooperation – relatively remote, mediate, dispensable, and so on – are permissible in specific cases, and this determination is not itself a matter of religion or conscientious belief. But these are all cases of coerced or compelled cooperation, where the person does not want to be involved but is put under pressure to do so. I have argued that their involvement can sometimes be justified even if they are thereby, to some relatively small degree, associated with the primary wrongdoing to which they object.

What I have in mind now is the thought that in a liberal society, people should generally not be put under pressure to be involved in any way with activities to which they have a conscientious objection. Moreover, this liberal duty reflects the broader freedom of dissociation that liberalism ought to accept as basic. In a free society, we generally do not expect either the government or other citizens to go about forcing or pressuring us to get involved in anything we do not want to get involved in. I have no right to pressure you to make friends with certain people rather than others. You have no right to pressure me to join this or that club or political party. I have no right to force you to go and watch the yearly Gay Pride parade. You have no right to force me to pray at the local mosque, church or synagogue.

This is all so obvious as hardly to seem worth stating. Yet the continued, and increasing, pressure on the consciences of people in health-related professions is, as it were, the 'canary in the coal mine' for the developing pressure on many people to act against their beliefs in other areas of social life. Whether it be using 'gender-neutral' bathrooms, hiding signs of religious affiliation (hijabs, crosses, veils, etc.), compulsory sex education in schools, or having to pay taxes that fund activities to which a taxpayer has serious moral objections, conscientious objectors find themselves increasingly hard pressed to live according to their beliefs. Here's a specific example. In 2007, the University of Delaware was forced by adverse publicity to drop a 'treatment' programme in residence halls for the ideological manipulation of students. Students were required to meet with advisers in order to answer questions such as 'when did you discover your sexual identity?', questions about their views on environmentalism, diversity, racism, and whether they were 'privileged' or 'oppressed'.[6] When one student was asked about their sexuality, they replied 'none of your damn business', as one might expect. This sort of intrusiveness into the beliefs and values of others may not yet be widespread, but the fact that anyone could even think it acceptable to make such an intrusion, to the point

---

6   https://www.thefire.org/cases/university-of-delaware-students
     -required-to-undergo-ideological-reeducation/ [last accessed 26.10.17].

where only an intense media campaign was able to force the University of Delaware to drop the programme, says something about the anti-liberal drift of the modern liberal state. Which is perhaps why freedom of dissociation needs more emphasis than ever.

In fact, the worry is even greater than I have portrayed it so far. Return to the case of *Bull v. Hall* – the Christian guest house owners who refused to rent a room to a gay couple. The UK Supreme Court ruled against the owners. Now, renting means selling a time-limited portion of one's property. In the case of a guest house, it also means selling whatever services come with rental of a room, such as making meals, cleaning the room, providing various amenities, and so on. So if the law requires a person to sell their goods and services to another person (under pain of severe financial penalty), even though they object on conscientious grounds to doing so, why shouldn't the law also require a person to work for another person even though they object, on conscientious grounds, to working for that person? After all, working for someone is just another contract of sale – the sale of one's labour. Moreover if the law, as it does, requires a person to hire another even though they object, on conscientious grounds, to doing so, why shouldn't it require someone to work for another despite conscientious objection? In other words, if you are compelled to sell your goods and services to someone despite conscientious objection, why not your labour? And if you are compelled to buy someone's labour despite such an objection, why shouldn't you be compelled to sell it? Yet being compelled by law to work for someone you don't want to work for is tantamount to a form of slavery, or at least forced labour.[7]

For what it is worth, forced labour has long been condemned by the International Labour Organization, in conventions dating back to 1930 and 1957.[8] The 1930 convention, ratified to date by 178 countries (i.e. virtually universally), condemns 'all work or service which is exacted from any person under the menace of any penalty and for which the said person has not offered himself voluntarily' (Forced Labour 1930: Article 2, sec. 1). The only exceptions are military service, 'normal civic obligations' including 'minor communal services', punishment for conviction in a court, and emergency service. Under 'normal civic obligations' one might include such paid or unpaid labour as jury service and assisting law enforcement, among others (National Academies 2004: 141). There is no suggestion that it includes routine employment. Further, the 1957 convention, ratified by 175 countries, explicitly condemns 'forced or compulsory labour' as 'a means of political coercion or education or as a punishment for holding or expressing political views or views ideologically opposed

---

7   It is interesting to note that, in law, the equitable remedy of specific performance is not available for contracts for personal services, in particular employment contracts. In the words of Fry LJ in *De Francesco v. Barnum* (1890) 45 Ch D 430: '...the courts are bound to be jealous, lest they should turn contracts of service into contracts of slavery.' (See Stockwell and Edwards 2005: 540.) One can make a slave without physically coercing them: one need only make the penalty for *not* working for a particular person heavy enough.

8   See http://www.ilo.org/global/about-the-ilo/newsroom/news/ WCMS_181922/lang--en/index.htm and the links therein to the two conventions [last accessed 26.10.17].

to the established political, social or economic system', and as 'as a means of racial, social, national or religious discrimination' (Abolition 1957: Article 1). On the face of it, it seems that being compelled to sell one's labour to a specific person or group despite a conscientious objection to doing so is ruled out under these conventions. Yet if one must sell one's goods and services, what is the difference?

If freedom of dissociation were given the force that it deserved, many of these sorts of problem could be obviated. A Christian couple could refuse to rent their room to a gay couple as long as there were other providers willing to supply a room. Why should it matter that there be other providers? In other words, why should freedom of dissociation depend upon whether one of the parties can have their wants fulfilled by a third party? The answer is that I am trying to find a practicable solution to the problem that respects both sides. Suppose Bill and Bob are starving and they come across one life-saving piece of food that, if divided between them, would not be enough to save either of them. Who should get the food, assuming there are no other factors to differentiate them in terms of entitlement? It looks as though, in a case such as this, morality has no answer. But it does, and the answer is – toss a coin. After all, to say that neither Bill nor Bob should have the food, and so both should die, seems morally repugnant. To say that both should have the food is morally impossible since it is physically impossible. To say that one should be preferred over the other, given no differentiating factor, seems objectionably arbitrary because ungrounded in any good reason. A coin toss looks like the only decent alternative:

if Bob wins the toss, then his getting the food is not objectionably arbitrary. This is because the coin toss is a way of *recognising* rather than denying the equal entitlement of both individuals. Random selection is precisely the reason for awarding the food to one rather than the other.

Return now to the case at hand. Suppose we were in the unlikely situation where the gay couple could not find another guest house that was sufficiently suitable to meet their needs, and there was no other compromise they could reasonably be asked to make (such as abiding by the rules of the Christian guest house or not taking a holiday in that area, or at that time, and so on). In that case, given the assumption that both sides had an equal entitlement to have their rights respected (an assumption I have been making all along), a coin toss looks like the only solution. If the Christian owners win, the gay couple does not get the room. If the gay couple wins, they do. We cannot say that freedom of dissociation should prevail because that would make one side a winner and the other a loser despite their equal entitlement. Hence the requirement that the gay couple should have a reasonable prospect of meeting their requirements in another way. Or, to put the point a little differently: the cases that are our concern are *not* like the situation of the starving Bill and Bob and the one piece of food. A (metaphorical) coin toss should not be necessary, since both sides *can* be accommodated. So they both should be.

Of course, what counts as a 'reasonable prospect' of someone's meeting their requirements in another way is going to be difficult to unpack. Minor inconvenience doesn't make a prospect unreasonable. Having to make a total change of plan does. Perhaps the devil is in the detail, but here I tend to think the details should not detain us. The main point is that if freedom of dissociation is to work effectively, all parties have to have a reasonable prospect of respect for their rights. In a conscience case, the objector must have a reasonable prospect of their conscientious objection being respected, and the opposing party must have a similar prospect of their rights being respected.

When monopoly is coercion

Monopolies are inherently coercive. This is because if you want a good or service, and it is monopolised, you have to purchase it from the monopoly supplier. We probably all agree that, in general, monopolies are an economically bad thing. But monopolies can also be morally bad, and not just because of inequity in the distribution of resources. Currently, the UK has a very small private market for health care. The National Health Service is a virtual monopoly supplier. This means that if you want to work as a doctor, nurse or other mainstream health practitioner, it is almost certain you will have to work for the NHS. The problem for religious freedom and freedom of conscience is that, as the midwives in *Doogan* found out, it is very hard to exercise your freedoms when you have no other place to go.

Suppose, however, that there were no (virtual) monopoly on health care. Suppose that a conscientious objector to, say, abortion, or extreme cosmetic surgery, or transgender surgery, or apotemnophilia (should it ever be approved by the

NHS), or 'neuro-enhancement', or eugenics – the list goes on and on – were able, due to 'full and fair access', to be free to exercise their profession at another hospital. Assuming the person wanting one of these services could get it, why shouldn't the objector be able to dissociate themselves from such a service and ply their trade without a troubled conscience? Again, I ask the question: in a liberal society, how could this not be morally required? Or, to put it less strongly: why, at least in principle, should such an arrangement be objectionable? There would be no need for piecemeal conscience clauses or ad hoc litigation, though of course cases would still need adjudication and a body of common-law precedent would need to develop. The situation would be in many respects similar to the US, where the federal Church Amendments[9] give extensive conscience protection to workers in hospitals in receipt of federal funding. Because there is a far more expansive private health sector in the US than in the UK, there is already far more employment choice and health-care workers can generally avoid getting into difficult conscience situations – ones that may arise whether or not there is any statutory protection for conscientious objection. Statutory protection should, I submit, be in place; full and fair access to relevant resources and facilities for both parties on the sides of a conscience case gives that protection an extra layer of substance. But even without it, a diverse and expansive private sector still gives conscientious objectors an important measure of *practical* security.

---

9   Church (1973). The Church Amendments are not named after any religious institution but after the senator who sponsored them.

The Satanist nurse

This brings us to some very difficult and delicate questions. I do not pretend to have all of the answers – I may have none of them – but these questions need to be discussed, and the problems they raise do not seem to me to undermine the general case I have been making either for freedom of conscience in the narrower sense or freedom of dissociation in the broader sense. I start with the hardest sorts of case, because if I can say something plausible about them, consistently with what I have been arguing as a whole, easier cases should be less troublesome.

Consider the Satanist nurse who refuses to treat Christians because it goes against her Satanist code of conduct. Should her conscientious objection be respected in law and policy? There are three reasons why the nurse might find herself in that situation: it was deliberate; it was an accident; it was necessary. If deliberate, i.e. the nurse wanted to be in a situation where she could refuse to administer life-saving treatment to a Christian, she would be no different to the diabolical serial killer nurses we occasionally hear about[10] – liable to prosecution for homicide. It is not as though I am suggesting current laws regarding crimes against the person should be changed to accommodate conscientious objection to not killing! Nor, as I have already suggested, should there be protection for a health-care worker who wants to refrain from

---

10 Such as a recent, gruesome case from Brazil: http://www.torontosun.com/ 2013/03/28/brazilian-doctor-charged-with-7-murders-linked-to-300 -deaths.

doing what is manifestly, on any reasonable interpretation, required by her strict professional duties. On the other hand, if the Satanist nurse was there by accident, she obviously did not know what she might be exposed to, so she lacked information. The remedy would be for every hospital to make it abundantly clear what kinds of treatment they provided and whether their patient base was universal or restricted.

The third reason is that the nurse had nowhere else to work and, knowing the problem she might face of having to treat a Christian, held her nose and went to work there anyway. The solution is obvious: she should not have to work there! On my proposal, she should not have to find another profession any more than the midwives Doogan and Wood. One might think that these 'outlier' cases would always be covered by what I said earlier – that there should be no conscience protection for objectors not wanting to be involved in activities that are manifestly 'part and parcel' of the medical profession. If so, then so much the better for my position. But I have in mind here cases that are not so easily dismissed in this way. Suppose the Satanist's views were bound up with her attitude to the ethics of euthanasia; suppose she had a story to tell about the need to let elderly and terminally ill Christians 'meet their Maker' rather than treat them, or some such. Rather, she would have the option of working in a private Satanist hospital where the Satanist code of conduct would be a precondition of employment and the hospital advertised quite clearly and unambiguously whom they treated and what services they offered. Needless to say, they should not expect a large clientele – many hard-headed Satanists would probably avoid it as well – but at least the nurse would have somewhere to ply her Satanic trade. Freedom of dissociation, though, should apply to individuals as well as groups: what if the nurse was, as it were, 'the only Satanist in the village'? That freedom of dissociation applies to individuals as well as groups does not imply that an individual can manage without a group to back them up. Conscientious objectors in wartime generally benefit from well-worked-out procedures enabling them to avoid violating their consciences, whether they be moved to medical work, administrative jobs, and so on. An individual pacifist may well feel himself alone but he knows that there will be others scattered about and many that have gone before him, and he can benefit from that shared history. By contrast, if there really were only one Satanist health-care worker with no Satanist support to rely on, it would, alas, be bad luck: if the person in that society is so idiosyncratic in their beliefs as to find themselves out on a limb, they might just have to make some sacrifices (so to speak). They might well have to retrain, or else leave the country. A small price to pay, I would say, for a right to dissociation.

Sex and race

The case of the Satanist nurse is pretty weird, I admit. Consider, though, cases involving race, gender or sexual orientation – all perennial hot button topics in liberal, pluralistic societies. As I have already suggested, for the law to impose financial penalties on Christian guest house owners for not renting their room to a gay couple is tantamount to compelling the sale of goods and services to particular customers. The same applies to Christian bakers being penalised for not selling a cake with a pro-homosexual message or for a gay wedding. True, the courts cannot *as things stand* order the objector to sell their wares or services to the other party. Still, a heavy (potentially un-limited) compensation order, along with the reputational damage and ancillary costs involved in being found guilty of breaching equality law, is as close to a kind of coercion as there can be short of ordering the sale to take place. But if the sale of goods and services can be forced, why not the sale of one's own *labour*? Yet that is slavery. And why can't the *purchase* of goods and services also be forced? If I were an atheist I wouldn't like to think I could be forced (say, by the threat of severe financial penalties) to buy a Bible from a religious believer selling them on the street on pain of religious discrimination. Yet what is the difference be-tween that case and the guest house apart from the irrel-evant one that the former involves purchase and the latter involves sale?

If we pursue this line of reasoning, what happens to freedom of contract, a pillar of the common law and a free society? Without freedom of contract, freedom of associa-tion is deprived of one of its central planks. Let us retrace our steps for a minute. I can imagine an objector thinking that at this point my argument is running out of control. Am I saying that freedom of association/dissociation and freedom of contract permit a person, *morally*, to decline to rent a room to another because of their race? Or their religion? Or their gender? Should we be going back to the bad old days when signs were found outside shops saying 'We don't serve blacks' or 'We don't serve Jews' or 'Irish need not apply'? If *that's* where my freedom of conscience/ freedom of dissociation argument is leading, then even if we can't see exactly what has gone wrong with it, we can be sure something has.

When it comes to, say, Christians, gays and guest houses, I do not think dissociation does seem repugnant on its face. In contemporary liberal society with a reasonably free market in goods and services, in fact, dissociation might lead to a thriving market in guest houses for gay couples (only gay and also mixed), and perhaps also in guest houses for Christians. There is no reason in advance for thinking that either group would not be catered for given the requirement – as I submit should be mandated by law – for 'full and fair access'. Yet when it comes to ethnicity, religion or gender (and perhaps other groupings) we tend to think immediately that old prejudices will rear their head and one group or other will end up with the short end of the straw. We think of certain groups being treated as 'second-class citizens' with access only to second-tier facilities. The history of this is regrettable, but a similar future is not inevitable: for instance, male-only clubs are still legal in the UK but there has been a surge in female-only clubs in upscale parts of London. It is still legal in the UK to refuse membership to a club or association on grounds of, among other characteristics, religion or ethnic origin, as long as the club is set up precisely for the purpose of restriction to the characteristic on the basis of which refusal of membership is made (Equality 2010).[11] So it is not inexorable that if some individuals or groups could not gain access to some facilities, all they would have left was a second-class remainder. There would have to be a societal demand for real *equality* of access; but access to equal services is not the same as equal access to services. Even if a second-class remainder was the result in a given case, why couldn't the government step in and mandate certain standards for all associations? They already do it for food retail, doctors' surgeries, sports facilities, and so on.

What kind of society?

An objector will probably claim that all my talk about full and fair access, and the usefulness of private markets, is completely missing the point. It is not, they will say, about second-class standards but about the kind of society we want to live in, about attitudes toward each other. If there were wholesale limitations on association available to any and every group and even every individual, what would this say about our common citizenry and about the 'inclusiveness' that is supposed to be the hallmark of a liberal, diverse, secular, tolerant, pluralistic society?

I understand the worry. But I also see how the issue of tolerance and respect cuts both ways. On the one hand, we show tolerance and respect by encouraging association among fellow citizens rather than discouraging it.

11 For explanation, see EHRC (2014: 20).

The governments of pluralistic societies, as well as many liberal-minded citizens, want people to be happy together, not apart. The desire is hardly unreasonable, and it would certainly be illiberal to encourage dissociation among people who do not want it. In other words, dissociation should not trump free association; rather, it is merely the converse of an existing right, and if the former is downgraded the latter ceases to be a mere right (if, as I claim, it is) and becomes something akin to an obligation. This looks like a recipe for friction rather than a social lubricant.

On the other hand, an essential element of tolerance and respect is the recognition that we all have certain freedoms in the way we organise our space of social interactions. A person or group might not wish to form a certain association because of a deep and sincerely held objection to involvement in an organisation that requires performance of certain actions violating their religious or ethical beliefs. Or, at the other end of the spectrum, they might simply not want to form a certain association due to personal or group preference. People do this sort of thing all the time, for example in the choice of where they live, where they work or where they send their children to school.

A given preference may or may not mask an attitude worthy of deprecation. I might not want to be your friend because I haven't noticed you, or have enough friends already. Such situations hardly involve reprehensible attitudes. It might also be that I suspect that you are untrustworthy or just plain boring. Here, attitudes are in play but they may be perfectly reasonable, founded on good evidence.

But they may also be honest beliefs founded on insufficient evidence yet without any cognitive irresponsibility on my part. Now suppose I don't like the colour of your hair, or don't want to be seen with you because I find you ugly, or I just don't like the colour of your skin. Probably all of us would see such attitudes as worthy of disapproval. Yet no law forces us to make friends with anyone, however bad our reasons for not doing so. It is hard, more importantly undesirable, to legislate against bad attitudes per se, and downright totalitarian to compel particular friendships whatever the reasons people have for not forming them. Although the law should reflect morality, morality and law are not the same. The mere fact that something is immoral does not make it something the law must punish. There are all kinds of acts and attitudes reasonable people criticise on moral grounds (rudeness, promise-breaking, unfriend-liness, lying) that are *not* punishable by law. So we can retain our moral criticism, and even use social pressure to change attitudes and dispositions to certain kinds of action, without thinking that it is the job of the law to enforce or punish them. If there is an overarching reason that is itself moral in nature – the importance of freedom of association and dissociation, for example – that may be grounds for not inserting the state and the legal system into other matters that are also moral in nature, such as acts and attitudes worthy of disapproval.

It is not clear to me why *civic friendship*, if I can put it that way, is especially different in this regard from personal friendship. We all have civic duties, of course, both to the state and to each other, and these require a certain amount of association. I have to associate with Her Majesty's Revenue and Customs to the extent necessary for me to pay my taxes. Absolutist tax protesters aside, we rightly find this sort of compelled association desirable. Whenever someone takes on a certain social role, or enters into certain communal activities having understood and tacitly accepted the rules surrounding those activities, they are to a degree compelled to associate with particular persons and groups rather than others. If you choose to shop in Sainsbury's, you had better accept the need to associate minimally with the other shoppers. If you choose to send your child to school X rather than school Y, you had better be ready to associate, perhaps to a relatively high degree, with the other parents as well as the teachers. This idea of tacit acceptance is important, and it clearly undergirds many of our social interactions. The critic of freedom of dissociation might object that civic friendship is disanalogous to personal friendship precisely due to this tacit acceptance. One does not have to be a social contract theorist about morality to recognize that there is a sense in which we have all 'signed up' to certain kinds of behaviour merely by dint of being a citizen of a certain state, whether or not we chose to be one.

For the purposes of the present discussion, what have we signed up to in virtue merely of being citizens rather than citizens who have adopted certain roles or social environments? We have signed up to the behaviour that inevitably comes with being civic associates – whether it be paying taxes, being good neighbours, obeying the law, keeping the peace, and so on. If we are capable of working and have no prior reason not to, we have signed up to being productive members of society. We have not, I contend, signed up to associating with any particular individual or group, though we have signed up to being, as it were, 'good associates' of both those with whom association is unavoidable in the circumstances and of whomever we have chosen to associate with in the first place. Other than that, I contend, we are – to put it in a slightly negative form – free to be left alone. I am not averse to calling the freedom of dissociation the 'right to be left alone' because this formulation wears on its face the notion of *personal space* – the freedom without which a person truly is a cog in a totalitarian regime. Personal space is not undermined by the simple requirement that when you do associate with other citizens, whether through choice or necessity, you are obliged to be civil to them – in the literal, etymological sense of the term. Only anarchists or sociopaths think that one's very presence in a state, living with its citizenry, is an affront to one's personal space. That space is undermined, in my view, by state-sanctioned requirements of *particular association.* Such requirements shrink one's personal space almost to vanishing point if applied across the board. If not applied across the board yet still applied broadly in a way that rubs increasingly against one's deeply held beliefs or even against one's simple personal and day-to-day choices – as is the case now – one's personal space is severely constrained and diminished.

7 POLICY GUIDELINES: TIME FOR PARLIAMENTS AND COURTS TO TAKE NOTICE

How to take freedom of conscience seriously without harming others

The previous chapter is clearly the most controversial and speculative part of what I have been arguing. I want to row back from that in this final chapter, considering more down-to-earth proposals for handling conscience issues in health care and to some extent beyond. And I want to make some brief points about freedom of dissociation at a very general level.

In the UK, the Equality Act 2010 is a massive statute designed to bring together all previous anti-discrimination laws. It has various curious features, one of which is section 1, *requiring* public sector bodies to consider ways to increase *equality of outcome* in respect of 'socio-economic disadvantage' when exercising their functions. Not mere equality of opportunity, but actual equality of outcome. For present purposes, it appears that public sector bodies, such as councils or government agencies, must take into account equality of outcome when determining which 'protected characteristic' overrides which others in an equality or discrimination case, at least when any 'socio-economic disadvantage' is at stake – and of course the latter term can be interpreted as widely as one likes. If a gay couple wants a wedding cake and a Christian baker refuses to supply it on religious or ethical grounds, then any public body somehow involved could be legally entitled to penalise the baker because the refusal would allegedly put the couple at a socio-economic disadvantage. The council might, for example, be legally allowed to deny planning permission to the baker for an extension to her shop until she rectified the disadvantage suffered by the gay couple, who were deprived of a particular service.

Why can't such a possible result, unfair and unequal in terms of basic rights, be turned around and the whole problem looked at in a more positive light? If a 'full and fair access' clause were written into the legislation, then government bodies could be placed under a statutory obligation not to penalise conscientious objectors, but to encourage and stimulate access to goods and services for those who would otherwise be disadvantaged. Consider again the men-only clubs in London. I have not checked whether any councils or other public sector bodies made it easier for women-only clubs to spring up as a result of their exclusion from men's clubs. But such bodies conceivably could work for that sort of outcome – by relaxing planning laws and by other incentives to make sure there was general access to a particular good, service or facility without compelling any particular person or provider to offer it or penalising anyone in particular for refusing it.

It might be that the Equality Act, and similar wide-ranging equality laws – such as the proposed US Equality Act, which died in Congress in 2015 – simply cannot be made to work in a way that *equally* protects all of the fundamental rights recognised in liberal society, in particular freedom of religion and conscience. Perhaps, for example, the fact that nearly all such legislation is framed in terms of 'discrimination' means that certain rights will always be interpreted by the courts, as in *Bull v. Hall* and *Ashers Baking Company*, in favour of those seeking a good or service rather than those providing it. If this more pessimistic outlook is correct, then perhaps wholesale repeal of the equality laws is the only solution. Note, however, that this need only apply to private individuals and groups as against each other, as well as to government bodies inasmuch as their actions directly affect private transactions. It could still be a requirement of government bodies in their actions that did not directly affect private transactions – in particular, government hiring – that such bodies did not discriminate against any particular rights holder because of some 'protected characteristic' they possessed. After all, it's not as though governments can be conscientious objectors against their own citizens, or that there is any analogue of freedom of religion or belief on the part of governments – at least in liberal societies. Governments or states cannot exercise freedom of dissociation against their citizens (except, I suppose, through exile), but only against other states or governments.

One might hope, though, that there was a way of reframing or reinterpreting the equality laws to put rights holders on a more level footing without wholesale repeal. For example, the usual 'provision of goods and services' clause could be replaced by a clause concerning the 'buying and selling of goods, services or labour'. In that case, someone seeking to buy goods would be, legally, on the same equality footing as someone seeking to sell them. Someone buying a service would be treated the same as someone selling their labour. You might object: but that is a recipe for irresistible forces meeting immovable objects! Person A, for instance, wants a service from person B. B has a conscientious objection to providing it. But A cannot be discriminated against when he seeks it. So how does my more all-encompassing clause help resolve anything?

Part of the answer lies in the concept of 'full and fair access'. If A has full and fair access to the service elsewhere, there can be no obligation on B to provide it if he really does object on conscience grounds. But why *should* A have to look elsewhere? Because of the other part of the answer, which concerns who approached whom. Freedom of dissociation should be, as I suggested earlier, thought of as something like a 'right to be left alone'. We all have a right to be left alone – in our homes, our private lives, our personal habits and amusements, and so on. The only question is whether the right to be left alone ends at a person's front gate. It seems to me irrational to think that it must end there. The idea of freedom of dissociation is supposed to give some flesh to the necessary, but somewhat uncomfortable, truth that sometimes the best way of getting along is by not getting along. Hence the 'full and fair access' clause in a given case should apply to the person or group who actively seeks the goods or services of another. The onus should be on the seeker to obtain alternative access, but the access must itself be full and fair. The onus should be on the state – and perhaps all of us in small or large ways – to ensure that such alternative access is always available without legal impediment. This, to my mind, is what 'full and fair access' means.

Does the UK need a Religious Freedom Restoration Act?

Something like the American RFRA is worth considering in the UK, at least to begin to redress the balance that currently swings away from religious believers. Any law or regulation placing a substantial burden on the free exercise of religion could only be justified if it passed 'strict scrutiny': was the burden the least restrictive means of implementing a compelling government interest? Compare this test to the one used (albeit in passing) by Lady Hale in *Bull v. Hall*: was 'the limitation on the right of Mr and Mrs Bull to manifest their religion ... a *proportionate* means of achieving a *legitimate* aim' (emphasis added) under the European Convention? (Bull 2013: 16). (Note that this wording is not in the Convention itself.) Given Lady Hale's own misgivings about whether a 'reasonable accommodation' has been found in the attempt to balance freedom of religion and conscience against other rights, perhaps she might reconsider what sort of test is best applied – although this would ultimately be a matter for legislators.

The point is that there is no way freedom of religion and conscience can adequately be protected if the mere fact that the government enacted a general law advancing some interest (whether a genuine interest or only something in which the government was interested) meant that this freedom had to take second place. If a law placed conscientious objectors under a substantial burden – including making them illicit cooperators according to recognised judicial principles – then the government would have to have a compelling interest in doing so, and it would have to do so in the least burdensome way practically available. It does not seem to me that the mere advancing of some competing right, on the part of an individual or group, could of itself constitute a compelling interest. The mere fact that the government considered an interest compelling would not make it so. Nor would an interest be compelling merely because some interest group, advocacy organisation, or other private or public body considered it so.

In a liberal society, the government is not supposed to play favourites. Rather, a compelling interest would have to stem from some overall societal need to, for example: (1) maintain social order and stability; (2) redress an existing imbalance or injustice in the way competing rights are treated; (3) ensure the smooth running of government; or (4) prevent direct harm to an individual or group. There may be other sources of compelling interests, but in a liberal society there could not be many.

Even if a compelling interest could be established, the government would have to find itself with virtually no other alternative but to impose the burden. Governments, however, are excellent at finding alternatives. If full and fair access was written into law, the government would have an obligation from the start to find ways of achieving its compelling interests without substantially burdening freedom of religion and conscience. It would have to concentrate, in the core of its policy-making and implementation, on preventing such burdens. It would have to be animated by a desire to find mechanisms and structures that enabled needs to be met without requiring people to act against their most deeply held beliefs.

General statutory guidelines

In 2015, a Private Member's Bill sponsored by Baroness O'Loan was introduced into the House of Lords to address conscientious objection in health care (O'Loan 2015). Although at the time of writing it is still formally in play, the bill is stuck in committee stage and may well be dead in the water. Still, it represents recognition by some legislators that there is a problem. Drafted in response to *Doogan*, the bill seeks to extend conscience protection beyond mere 'treatment' under the Abortion Act to 'any activity under the provisions of the Abortion Act 1967, including activity required to prepare for, support or perform termination of pregnancy.' It also adds provisions concerning 'withdrawal of life-sustaining treatment' and activities related to the ever increasing, and legal, experimentation on human embryos.

The bill is not nearly adequate, of course – only an early draft designed, unsuccessfully thus far, to get the legislative ball rolling. That said, it points the way to what ought to be done legislatively to give conscience protection in health care the foundation it currently lacks. A similar attempt was made in the US House of Representatives in 2011, with the Respect for Rights of Conscience Bill, drafted in response the Obamacare mandates discussed earlier (Fortenberry 2011). Here, the aim was to give conscience protection to individuals and health insurers from being required to 'provide, participate in, or refer for a specific item or service contrary to the provider's religious beliefs or moral convictions.' As with the UK bill, the American one has languished.

If we are to avoid piecemeal protections, as I submit we should, then we need legislation that is broader than these examples – something with the scope of, and perhaps even written into, all equality laws. For example: 'no individual, whether through their own agency or the agency of a corporation or other legally recognised body, shall be required to provide, participate in, cooperate with, or refer for, any goods or services of a health-care-related nature contrary to that individual's conscientious beliefs, religious beliefs or moral convictions'.

Should 'legally recognised bodies' be confined to the private sector? There are two ways we could go here. Strictly, liberal states are not supposed to play favourites. In which case they should respect, even in their own governmental agencies, the conscience of a Christian or Muslim, say, as much as the legal right of someone to an abortion or a medical examination. Many Christians oppose abortion. Many Muslim doctors do not believe in intimately examining patients of the opposite sex.[12] On the other hand, as I have argued, full and fair access and the absence of monopoly providers would leave it open for the government to play favourites in its own agencies without substantially burdening health-care workers who came out second best in any conflict of rights. I am not sure much hangs on which option is preferred: as long as freedom of conscience is protected, either is viable.

The role of case law

Any statutory framework protecting freedom of conscience needs to be quite general. The sample provision I have just given includes the term 'cooperation', but it would be a mistake to require parliament to define that term. Common law is replete with what might be called 'terms of art' such as 'negligent', 'cause', 'foreseeable', 'reasonable', and the like. Rarely if ever do legislators try to define such terms, partly because they are so broad and generic that any definition would, for legal purposes, be itself so wide in scope as to be of little practical use. In addition, the breadth of the terms means that they crop up all over the common law, in just about any kind of tort case you could think of, as well as contract, property, and other areas. Their wide applicability means that a huge range of types of factual situation can be relevant to how those terms are applied, and it is hard to tell in advance how a given term might be

---

12 In a recent survey of medical students, 36 per cent of Muslims said they would object to performing an intimate examination of a patient of the opposite sex (Strickland 2012).

employed in a particular case. So, in their wisdom, parliaments leave it to judges to give flesh to the bare bones of these very general legal concepts.

It is the wisdom of the judges to which we should be looking for interpretation of a term such as 'cooperation', but they would have to be informed by jurisprudence on the matter. I outlined earlier a plausible theory that focuses on concepts such as proximity of cooperation, dispensability, formal versus material cooperation, and the balancing of good and bad outcomes. It might derive from a tradition of moral theology, but in itself it has no specifically theological content. Were judges to take proper judicial notice of such a theory (as opposed to the passing reference in *Hobby Lobby*), they would have the conceptual machinery to assess whether a given conscientious objector was being placed in a position of having to cooperate illicitly – by the lights of the theory – with some activity. Hence 'cooperation', in any general statutory clauses, would have to mean 'illicit' by implication, and what is illicit would be determined by judges using the theory, with a large helping of logic, common sense and the prudence for which the best common law judges are rightly famed.

Over time, a body of case law on cooperation would develop, with all the machinery of judicial precedent behind it. Certain kinds of case would crop up repeatedly in litigation, but many cases would never get to court because precedent was already clear. For an extreme example, the mere threat of losing a day's pay is enough to justify remote, dispensable cooperation in abortion, such as maintaining hygiene on an abortion ward. By contrast, it would take a very grave reason – a threat to one's very livelihood, say – to justify booking patients in for potentially very harmful cosmetic surgery done for purely aesthetic reasons.

Be that as it may, I am confident that judges would be able to develop a rich case law of cooperation that bolstered freedom of conscience without giving it unrestricted scope. This will not satisfy all advocates of freedom of conscience, but I suspect that many who are not satisfied – such as the objectors in the *Little Sisters* case in the US, who considered an opt-out to be itself illicit cooperation – are really objecting to the very primary act with which they consider themselves to be potential cooperators. If they do not want even to sign a document opting out of, say, providing health insurance for contraceptives, it shows that what they are objecting to is contraception itself, or whatever activity is at the focus of the complaint. Such objectors have other avenues for protesting laws they consider immoral or unjust.

Sincerity is not enough

Which brings me back to the question of sincerity. In a liberal, pluralistic society, courts do not second-guess religious or ethical beliefs. They do not subject them to a test of reasonableness. As long as a belief is sincerely held (rather than seeming to be held as a pretext for avoiding the force of some general law, or for some other ulterior motive), the courts take it at face value. This may have inherent problems of its own, since beliefs can be outlandish and risible by any reasonable standard, and they can have a direct impact on non-adherents to the particular code or system from which they derive. But that is a discussion for another occasion. Working within the framework we currently have in most Western countries for protecting religious freedom, we have to accept that sincerity is enough when it comes to religious and ethical beliefs.

Where sincerity is not enough, however, is in the determination of how involved a conscientious objector may be in the actions of others, given the objector's sincere beliefs. This, I claim, is a matter for reasonable judgment using philosophical principles of cooperation. An objector's mere claim that they are illicitly involved, or compromised, by assisting however remotely with some primary act to which they object cannot be taken at face value. This can no more be a matter of mere sincerity than a litigant's belief that they were treated by some other party negligently, unjustly or unreasonably. These are matters for courts to determine, and involvement by cooperation is in the same category.

The fact that a court may, for example, determine that a conscientious objector is not substantially burdened because their cooperation is too remote does not, however, entail that their cooperation is *obligatory*. It only means that their cooperation is *permissible*. This is part of the ethical theory of cooperation, which is about when cooperation is allowed even though it assists someone else to do something objectionable. This distinction should, I submit, be reflected in law. All things being equal, if an objector's proposed cooperation was permissible according to the sort of jurisprudence of cooperation I am recommending, a legal requirement to cooperate would not amount to a substantial burden on freedom of conscience.

All things might not, however, be equal. Courts need to have some leeway in letting a conscientious objector 'off the hook', as it were, even though their cooperation would be strictly permissible. Suppose the objector also believed that causing scandal was a serious wrong according to their system of belief. They might think that by cooperating, even remotely, in some wrongful act they were 'sending the wrong message' to fellow believers, or maybe even society at large. The belief that causing scandal was wrong would be a primary religious or ethical belief, part of the objector's system of beliefs. It, too, could not be second-guessed by the courts. All a court would have to do would be to determine whether, in fact, cooperation *would* cause scandal or send the wrong message. If so, then a conscientious objector might be found to be substantially burdened in *this* way, even though cooperation itself was not found to be a substantial burden. So, in protecting freedom of religion or conscience, the court might still be in a position to give the objector some kind of accommodation, allowing them to opt out of that to which they were objecting.

The broader lesson is that if freedom of conscience and religion is to have any real substance in a liberal, pluralistic society such as ours, it must have what it now lacks – not only a proper statutory framework but a worked-out jurisprudence that can guide the courts in giving conscientious objectors the protection to which they are entitled.

Conclusion

Religious believers are currently mounting defensive operations to secure what little protection they have left in societies that are, by any fair measure, becoming increasingly secular and largely hostile to religious attitudes. And conscientious objection in general – whether religiously based or not – is coming under equal pressure in the face of a societal agenda that is less and less liberal, and more and more 'secular authoritarian', to put it tendentiously. Many will disagree with this view of things. Yet many will agree with me at least to some extent, and there will be all sorts of views as to how to deal with the problem.

If you do think there is a problem for freedom of religion and conscience in contemporary liberal society, then I hope you will agree with at least the central proposals I have made in this monograph:

1. In the UK and US, and probably in most similarly liberal, pluralistic and relatively secular societies, freedom of religion and freedom of conscience generally need to be put on a sound statutory footing that is more substantial than what we have now.
2. These freedoms extend not only to direct participation in actions that violate the beliefs of conscientious objectors, but also to cooperation with such actions.
3. Conscientious objectors face legal pressures to engage both in participation and in cooperation with activities that violate their beliefs.

4. There is a reasonable way – not essentially theological in character, even though emanating from a tradition of theological analysis – of assessing cases that can distinguish between permissible and impermissible forms of cooperation.

5. This method should be adopted by the courts in assessing whether, in cooperation cases, freedom of religion and conscience has been violated. It should be left to the wisdom and good sense of judges to build up a body of relevant case law.

REFERENCES

Abolition (1957) Abolition of Forced Labour Convention (http://www.ilo.org/dyn/normlex/en/f?p=NORMLEXPUB:12100:0::NO::P12100_INSTRUMENT_ID:312250) [last accessed 28.10.17].

Abortion (1967) Abortion Act UK (http://www.legislation.gov.uk/ukpga/1967/87) [last accessed 28.10.17].

All Party (2016) A Report by the All Party Parliamentary Pro-Life Group into Freedom of Conscience in Abortion Provision (https://adflegal.blob.core.windows.net/international-content/docs/default-source/default-document-library/resources/media-resources/europe/final-report-parliamentary-inquiry-into-freedom-of-conscience-in-abortion-provision-all-party-parliamentary-pro-life-group.pdf?sfvrsn=2) [last accessed 28.10.17].

Ashers (2016) *Gareth Lee v. Colin McArthur, Karen McArthur and Ashers Baking Company Limited* (http://www.bailii.org/nie/cases/NICA/2016/39.html) [last accessed 28.10.17].

Bland (1993) *Airedale National Health Service Trust v. Bland*, [1993] 1 All ER 821.

Bull (2013) *Bull v. Hall* (https://www.supremecourt.uk/cases/docs/uksc-2012-0065-judgment.pdf) [last accessed 28.10.17].

Burwell (2014) *Burwell, Secretary of State of Health and Human Services, et al. v. Hobby Lobby Stores, Inc., et al.* (https://www

.supremecourt.gov/opinions/13pdf/13-354_olp1.pdf)
[last accessed 28.10.17]. (Page references are to the pdf of the
slip opinion cited here.)

Church (1973) The Church Amendments (http://www.usccb
.org/issues-and-action/religious-liberty/conscience
-protection/upload/Federal-Conscience-Laws.pdf)
[last accessed 28.10.17].

Doogan (2014) *Greater Glasgow Health Board (Appellant) v.
Doogan and another (Respondents) (Scotland)* [2014] UKSC
68 (https://www.supremecourt.uk/decided-cases/docs/
UKSC_2013_0124_Judgment.pdf) [last accessed 28.10.17].
(Page references are to the pdf of the judgment cited here.)

EHRC (2014) Equality and Human Rights Commission, *What
equality law means for your association, club or society*
(https://www.equalityhumanrights.com/sites/default/files/
what_equality_law_means_for_your_association2c_club
_or_society.pdf) [last accessed 28.10.17].

Equality (2010) Equality Act UK (http://www.legislation.gov
.uk/ukpga/2010/15/contents) [last accessed 28.10.17].

European Council (2013) *EU Guidelines on the promotion and
protection of freedom of religion or belief* (https://eeas.europa
.eu/sites/eeas/files/137585.pdf) [last accessed 28.10.17].

FAFCE (2013) *Federation of Catholic Families in Europe (FAFCE)
v. Sweden* (https://rm.coe.int/CoERMPublicCommonSearch
Services/DisplayDCTMContent?documentId=090000168058
d2e9#search=fafce) [last accessed 28.10.17].

Forced Labour (1930) Forced Labour Convention (http://www
.ilo.org/dyn/normlex/en/f?p=NORMLEXPUB:12100:0::NO
::P12100_INSTRUMENT_ID:312174) [last accessed 28.10.17].

Fortenberry (2011) Respect for Rights of Conscience Act of 2011 (https://www.congress.gov/bill/112th-congress/house-bill/1179/text) [last accessed 28.10.17].

GPhC (2016) General Pharmaceutical Council, Consultation on Religion, Personal Values and Beliefs (https://www.pharmacyregulation.org/sites/default/files/consultation_on_religion_personal_values_and_beliefs_december_2016_0.pdf) [last accessed 28.10.17].

Hale, B. (2014) Annual Human Rights Lecture for the Law Society of Ireland: 'Freedom of Religion and Belief' (https://www.supremecourt.uk/docs/speech-140613.pdf) [last accessed 28.10.17].

Hernandez (1989) *Hernandez v. Commissioner of Internal Revenue*, 490 U.S. 680.

HFEA (1990) Human Fertilisation and Embryology Act UK (http://www.legislation.gov.uk/ukpga/1990/37/contents) [last accessed 5.5.18].

Hobby Lobby (2013) *Hobby Lobby Stores, Inc. v. Kathleen Sebelius* (https://www.ca10.uscourts.gov/opinions/12/12-6294.pdf) [last accessed 28.10.17]. (Page references are to the pdf of the slip opinion cited here.)

Little Sisters (2015) *Little Sisters of the Poor v. Burwell* (https://www.aclu.org/sites/default/files/field_document/07.14.15_little_sisters_opinion.pdf), 794 F.3d 1151 [last accessed 28.10.17]. (All references to pages in the judgment are to the slip opinion (header pagination).)

McFarlane (2010) *McFarlane v. Relate Avon Ltd* (http://www.bailii.org/ew/cases/EWCA/Civ/2010/880.html) [last accessed 28.10.17].

McHugh, J. A. and Callan, C. J. (1958) *Moral Theology: A Complete Course*, vol. 1. New York: Joseph F. Wagner, Inc.

National Academies (2004) Committee on Monitoring International Labor Standards, National Research Council of the National Academies, *Monitoring International Labor Standards: Techniques and Sources of Information*. Washington, DC: National Academies Press (https://www.nap.edu/catalog/10937/monitoring-international-labor-standards-techniques-and-sources-of-information) [last accessed 28.10.17].

Oderberg, D. S. (2003) The ethics of co-operation in wrongdoing. Royal Institute of Philosophy Annual Lecture Series 2002–3, pp. 203–27. Also in *Modern Moral Philosophy* (ed. A. O'Hear). Cambridge University Press (2004).

Oderberg, D. S. (2017a) Further clarity on cooperation and morality. *Journal of Medical Ethics* 43: 192–200.

Oderberg, D. S. (2017b) Cooperation in the age of *Hobby Lobby*: when sincerity is not enough. *Expositions* 11: 15–30 (https://expositions.journals.villanova.edu/pages/view/EIF) [last accessed 28.10.17].

Ogilvie, K. and Oliphant, R. (2016), *Medical Assistance in Dying: A Patient-Centred Approach*, Parliament of Canada, Report of the Special Joint Committee on Physician-Assisted Dying. (http://www.parl.gc.ca/content/hoc/Committee/421/PDAM/Reports/RP8120006/pdamrp01/pdamrp01-e.pdf) [last accessed 28.10.17].

O'Loan, N. (2016) Conscientious Objection (Medical Activities) Bill [HL] 2015-16 (http://services.parliament.uk/bills/2015-16/conscientiousobjection.html) [last accessed 28.10.17].

Orr, J. (2016) *Beyond Belief: Defending Religious Liberty through the British Bill of Rights*. London: ResPublica Trust (http://www.respublica.org.uk/our-work/publications/beyond-belief-defending-religious-liberty-british-bill-rights/) [last accessed 28.10.17].

Pichon (2001) *Pichon and Sajous v. France* (http://hudoc.echr.coe.int/eng?i=001-22644) [last accessed 28.10.17].

Poland (2011) *R.R. v. Poland* (http://hudoc.echr.coe.int/eng?i=001-104911#{%22itemid%22:[%22001-104911%22]}) [last accessed 28.10.17].

Priests for Life (2015) *Priests for Life v. US Department of Health and Human Services* (http://law.justia.com/cases/federal/appellate-courts/cadc/13-5368/13-5368-2015-05-20.html) [last accessed 28.10.17].

Rawls, J. (1993) *Political Liberalism*. New York: Columbia University Press.

RFRA (1993) Religious Freedom Restoration Act USA (https://www.law.cornell.edu/uscode/text/42/2000bb–1) [last accessed 28.10.17].

Stockwell, N. and Edwards, R. (2005) *Trusts and Equity*, 7th edn. Harlow: Pearson Education.

Strickland, S. (2012) Conscientious objection in medical students: a questionnaire survey. *Journal of Medical Ethics* 38: 22–25.

Thomas (1981) *Thomas v. Review Board of the Indiana Employment Security Division*, 450 U.S. 707.

Uehiro (2016) Consensus Statement on Conscientious Objection in Health Care (http://blog.practicalethics.ox.ac.uk/2016/08/consensus-statement-on-conscientious-objection-in-health care/) [last accessed 28.10.17].

Welsh (1970) *Welsh v. United States*, 398 U.S. 333 (1970) (https://supreme.justia.com/cases/federal/us/398/333/case.html#335) [last accessed 28.10.17].

Zubik (2016) *Zubik v. Burwell* (https://www.supremecourt.gov/opinions/15pdf/14-1418_8758.pdf) [last accessed 28.10.17].

ABOUT THE IEA

The Institute is a research and educational charity (No. CC 235 351), limited by guarantee. Its mission is to improve understanding of the fundamental institutions of a free society by analysing and expounding the role of markets in solving economic and social problems.

The IEA achieves its mission by:

- a high-quality publishing programme
- conferences, seminars, lectures and other events
- outreach to school and college students
- brokering media introductions and appearances

The IEA, which was established in 1955 by the late Sir Antony Fisher, is an educational charity, not a political organisation. It is independent of any political party or group and does not carry on activities intended to affect support for any political party or candidate in any election or referendum, or at any other time. It is financed by sales of publications, conference fees and voluntary donations.

In addition to its main series of publications, the IEA also publishes (jointly with the University of Buckingham), *Economic Affairs*.

The IEA is aided in its work by a distinguished international Academic Advisory Council and an eminent panel of Honorary Fellows. Together with other academics, they review prospective IEA publications, their comments being passed on anonymously to authors. All IEA papers are therefore subject to the same rigorous independent refereeing process as used by leading academic journals.

IEA publications enjoy widespread classroom use and course adoptions in schools and universities. They are also sold throughout the world and often translated/reprinted.

Since 1974 the IEA has helped to create a worldwide network of 100 similar institutions in over 70 countries. They are all independent but share the IEA's mission.

Views expressed in the IEA's publications are those of the authors, not those of the Institute (which has no corporate view), its Managing Trustees, Academic Advisory Council members or senior staff.

Members of the Institute's Academic Advisory Council, Honorary Fellows, Trustees and Staff are listed on the following page.

The Institute gratefully acknowledges financial support for its publications programme and other work from a generous benefaction by the late Professor Ronald Coase.

The Institute of Economic Affairs
2 Lord North Street, Westminster, London SW1P 3LB
Tel: 020 7799 8900
Fax: 020 7799 2137
Email: iea@iea.org.uk
Institute of
Economic Affairs   Internet: iea.org.uk

Other books recently published by the IEA include:

Selfishness, Greed and Capitalism: Debunking Myths about the Free Market
Christopher Snowdon
Hobart Paper 177; ISBN 978-0-255-36677-9; £12.50

Waging the War of Ideas
John Blundell
Occasional Paper 131; ISBN 978-0-255-36684-7; £12.50

Brexit: Directions for Britain Outside the EU
Ralph Buckle, Tim Hewish, John C. Hulsman, Iain Mansfield and
Robert Oulds
Hobart Paperback 178; ISBN 978-0-255-36681-6; £12.50

Flaws and Ceilings – Price Controls and the Damage They Cause
Edited by Christopher Coyne and Rachel Coyne
Hobart Paperback 179; ISBN 978-0-255-36701-1; £12.50

*Scandinavian Unexceptionalism: Culture, Markets and the Failure of
Third-Way Socialism*
Nima Sanandaji
Readings in Political Economy 1; ISBN 978-0-255-36704-2; £10.00

Classical Liberalism – A Primer
Eamonn Butler
Readings in Political Economy 2; ISBN 978-0-255-36707-3; £10.00

Federal Britain: The Case for Decentralisation
Philip Booth
Readings in Political Economy 3; ISBN 978-0-255-36713-4; £10.00

Forever Contemporary: The Economics of Ronald Coase
Edited by Cento Veljanovski
Readings in Political Economy 4; ISBN 978-0-255-36710-3; £15.00

Power Cut? How the EU Is Pulling the Plug on Electricity Markets
Carlo Stagnaro
Hobart Paperback 180; ISBN 978-0-255-36716-5; £10.00

Policy Stability and Economic Growth – Lessons from the Great Recession
John B. Taylor
Readings in Political Economy 5; ISBN 978-0-255-36719-6; £7.50

Breaking Up Is Hard To Do: Britain and Europe's Dysfunctional Relationship
Edited by Patrick Minford and J. R. Shackleton
Hobart Paperback 181; ISBN 978-0-255-36722-6; £15.00

In Focus: The Case for Privatising the BBC
Edited by Philip Booth
Hobart Paperback 182; ISBN 978-0-255-36725-7; £12.50

Islamic Foundations of a Free Society
Edited by Nouh El Harmouzi and Linda Whetstone
Hobart Paperback 183; ISBN 978-0-255-36728-8; £12.50

The Economics of International Development: Foreign Aid versus Freedom for the World's Poor
William Easterly
Readings in Political Economy 6; ISBN 978-0-255-36731-8; £7.50

Taxation, Government Spending and Economic Growth
Edited by Philip Booth
Hobart Paperback 184; ISBN 978-0-255-36734-9; £15.00

Universal Healthcare without the NHS: Towards a Patient-Centred Health System
Kristian Niemietz
Hobart Paperback 185; ISBN 978-0-255-36737-0; £10.00

Sea Change: How Markets and Property Rights Could Transform the Fishing Industry
Edited by Richard Wellings
Readings in Political Economy 7; ISBN 978-0-255-36740-0; £10.00

Working to Rule: The Damaging Economics of UK Employment Regulation
J. R. Shackleton
Hobart Paperback 186; ISBN 978-0-255-36743-1; £15.00

Education, War and Peace: The Surprising Success of Private Schools in War-Torn Countries
James Tooley and David Longfield
ISBN 978-0-255-36746-2; £10.00

Killjoys: A Critique of Paternalism
Christopher Snowdon
ISBN 978-0-255-36749-3; £12.50

Financial Stability without Central Banks
George Selgin, Kevin Dowd and Mathieu Bédard
ISBN 978-0-255-36752-3; £10.00

Against the Grain: Insights from an Economic Contrarian
Paul Ormerod
ISBN 978-0-255-36755-4; £15.00

Other IEA publications

Comprehensive information on other publications and the wider work of the IEA can be found at www.iea.org.uk. To order any publication please see below.

Personal customers

Orders from personal customers should be directed to the IEA:

Clare Rusbridge
IEA
2 Lord North Street
FREEPOST LON10168
London SW1P 3YZ
Tel: 020 7799 8907. Fax: 020 7799 2137
Email: sales@iea.org.uk

Trade customers

All orders from the book trade should be directed to the IEA's distributor:

NBN International (IEA Orders)
Orders Dept.
NBN International
10 Thornbury Road
Plymouth PL6 7PP
Tel: 01752 202301, Fax: 01752 202333
Email: orders@nbninternational.com

IEA subscriptions

The IEA also offers a subscription service to its publications. For a single annual payment (currently £42.00 in the UK), subscribers receive every monograph the IEA publishes. For more information please contact:

Clare Rusbridge
Subscriptions
IEA
2 Lord North Street
FREEPOST LON10168
London SW1P 3YZ
Tel: 020 7799 8907, Fax: 020 7799 2137
Email: crusbridge@iea.org.uk